Wagner

HIS LIFE & MUSIC

Stephen Johnson

sourcebooks
mediaFusion

An Imprint of
Sourcebooks Inc.®
Naperville, Illinois

© 2008 by Naxos Rights International Ltd
Cover and internal design © 2008 by Sourcebooks, Inc.
Cover photo © Corbis

Published by Sourcebooks MediaFusion, an imprint of Sourcebooks, Inc.
P.O. Box 4410, Naperville, Illinois 60567-4410
(630) 961-3900
Fax: (630) 961-2168
www.sourcebooks.com

Originally published in the UK by Naxos Books.
Library of Congress Cataloging-in-Publication Data

Johnson, Stephen
  Wagner : his life and music / by Stephen Johnson.
     p. cm.
  "Originally published in the UK by Naxos Books."
  Includes bibliographical references (p.   ) and index.
  1. Wagner, Richard, 1813-1883. 2. Composers--Germany--Biography. I. Title.

ML410.W1J64 2008
782.1092--dc22
[B]
                                    2007025790

              Printed and bound in the United States of America.
                   LT 10 9 8 7 6 5 4 3 2 1

Contents

www.naxos.com/naxosbooks/wagnerlifeandmusicusa

Visit the dedicated website for *Wagner: His Life and Music* and gain free access to the following:

- **Hours more music to listen to – historical and modern recordings**
- **Music by some of Wagner's contemporaries**
- **A timeline of Wagner's life, set alongside contemporary events in arts, culture and politics**

To access this you will need:

- **ISBN: 9781843792000**
- **Password: Nibelung**

On CD One

For more information on these tracks, see page 224.

v

On CD Two

For more information on these tracks, see page 227.

Preface

Even today, in a culture where classical music often appears to be desperately marginalized, the name Richard Wagner possesses a powerful resonance. *Ride of the Valkyries*, originally the opening of Act Three of the opera *Die Walküre*, remains one of the few pieces of orchestral music that most people seem able to recognize. How much this has to do with Copolla's famous use of it in his film *Apocalypse Now* is not easy to say, but when English National Opera performed the complete third act of *Die Walküre* at the Glastonbury pop festival it created an interest that surprised even some of its promoters. More than that, the adjective 'Wagnerian' carries an associative charge for people who would never think of setting foot in an opera house or buying a classical CD. I recently saw a school production of Oscar Wilde's *The Importance of Being Earnest* in which a mostly teenage audience roared with appreciative laughter at Algernon's line on hearing the doorbell sound in Act One: 'Ah! that must be Aunt Augusta. Only relatives, or creditors, ever ring in that Wagnerian manner.'

Clearly the word still means something, even if for some it is little more than 'grandiose' or 'overly insistent'. References to the immense *Ring* cycle in several recent high-profile stand-up comedy routines also suggest that many are still aware that Wagner created the most ambitious work in the history of western music: a cycle of four operas, using vast orchestral forces, demanding four separate evenings to perform, and requiring of its audience an almost religious attentiveness and devotion. It is also clear that today's rock musicians and journalists expect at least some of their listeners and readers to understand the meaning of the word 'leitmotif' – even if they cannot give a single example from the work of the man who pioneered that innovatory technique.

Inevitably there is another, much darker association with Wagner's name. In an age with an apparently insatiable demand for books or TV documentaries about the Third Reich, Wagner appears to be fixed in people's minds as 'Hitler's favorite composer'. That Hitler's enthusiasm for Wagner seems to have waned in his last years, that the dictator had reservations about Wagner's last opera *Parsifal* and that many fellow Nazis found Wagner boring or (more interestingly) ideologically suspect doesn't appear to have filtered through into the general consciousness. Wagner is also – justly – notorious for his anti-Semitism. There is no possible excuse for this aspect of his ideology, nor is there any way of diminishing its terrible significance for posterity. The fact that such views were commonplace in the latter half of the nineteenth century – and not only in Wagner's Germany – may help us to appreciate their context, and thus realize that they were not merely a bizarre personal aberration; but such understanding does nothing to soften the virulence of some of Wagner's written and reported comments. Racist paranoia was clearly an important feature of Wagner's personality, though there is evidence (discussed further in the 'Life' section of this book) that in some corner of his mind, even he may have realized that it was unworthy of him.

For all Wagner's notoriety, however, contemporary journalism and more general media comment makes it clear that the name Wagner carries other, less pejorative overtones. The scale of his ambition, and the extraordinary single-mindedness with which he carried it through, still excites admiration, however grudging. There also seems to be a lingering awareness that his operas – or, as he later preferred to call them, 'music dramas' – offer a degree of seriousness, and perhaps of psychological insight, that sets them apart from most of the standard operatic repertory: that, for instance, *Tristan und Isolde* is no ordinary operatic love story, but a searing account of the agonies and ecstasies of human desire. One of the main purposes of this book is to show, in terms accessible to the ordinary listener, that this reputation is justified. With the sole exception of Mozart, Wagner is the nearest thing that opera possesses to a Shakespeare. The comparison goes way beyond questionable categories of artistic 'rank'. One of the most fascinating things about Shakespeare's plays is the way that his characters often take on a life of their own – to the point where, as the novelist E.M. Forster put it, they 'get out of hand'. Shylock in *The Merchant of Venice* starts out in the play as a pasteboard 'grasping Jew' – a stock figure virtually guaranteed to set an Elizabethan theatre audience booing as soon as he appeared on the stage. Yet Shylock's great Act Three speech 'I am a Jew. Hath not a Jew eyes?' appeals so strongly to our common humanity that it turns the play morally on its head, and leaves an uncomfortable aftertaste long after the prettily contrived 'happy ending'.

Something similar can be sensed in Wagner's operas. Several writers have argued that the power- and gold-crazed dwarf Alberich in the *Ring* is an anti-Semitic caricature, and almost certainly there is truth in this allegation. But the scene in *Das Rheingold* in which Alberich is tricked out of his magical treasure by the gods Wotan and Loge is one of the most uncomfortable moments in the entire cycle – as Wagner clearly intended it to be. This is when we realize the extent to which power has corrupted Wotan himself, and see that the downfall of his regime is the only possible consequence. Wagner privately confessed that he felt pity for Alberich at this point, and his music makes this all too clear. And unlike *The Merchant of Venice*, the *Ring* offers no final justification for Wotan's actions. The gods' treatment of Alberich is simply a great wrong, and one that has consequences literally to the end of time.

For me, it was the experience of hearing *Parsifal* again in the legendary Hans Knappertsbusch recording that made me realize how important it is to identify the best in Wagner, and to show how it transcends and diminishes the worst. There may be – as some have argued – sinister racial overtones behind the image of the holy blood invoked in *Parsifal*, but most modern listeners have to be told that the message is there to be able to recognize it: Wagner never makes it explicit. More to the point, it surely pales beside the wonderful elevation of compassion as the power that not only outfaces evil but offers integration and enlightenment to the divided modern soul. For most listeners, the opera's roots in Christian and Buddhist notions of self-transcendence eclipse whatever the libretto may or may not owe to nineteenth-century racial theorists such as the once infamous Count Gobineau. All this is only served and strengthened by the ingenuity and heartrending beauty of Wagner's music.

That we need such a message today is starkly evident from every international newscast. So while this book makes no effort to gloss over the less pleasant aspects of Wagner's personality and thinking, its main purpose is to show that what matters most about Wagner's work are the very aspects that make it greater than the man – a fact that Wagner himself seems to have recognized, however dimly and intermittently. Some readers may come away from this book and its accompanying CDs and website feeling that their relationship with this titanic figure will always be something of a love–hate affair. If so, they have my very real sympathy. In any case, blind devotion is the last thing I want to encourage. If, however, this book also manages to give some indication of how much there is in Wagner that is truly worthy of love and admiration, then that can only be to the good.

About the CDs

In selecting and ordering the extracts on these CDs, my purpose was partly to give the reader a flavor of the main works under discussion in the 'Music' section of the book. I was also concerned that both discs should form a potentially enjoyable experience if played complete. For this reason the extracts are arranged not chronologically, but more like items in a concert program, where balance and contrast are at least as important as any didactic purpose. In any case, their relation to the text should be clear enough.

The
Life

Chapter 1

A Child of His Time

A Child of His Time

When Richard Wagner was born in Leipzig, on May 22, 1813, Europe was in the midst of convulsive change. The process accelerated dizzyingly in the months following his birth. Whether the newborn Wagner was in any way aware of the terror and carnage that soon erupted around him is impossible to say, but it helped to create the cultural climate in which he was brought up, and which left its imprint deep within him. In the year before Wagner arrived in the world, Napoleon, buoyed up by his triumphs across the continent, had mounted his catastrophic campaign against Russia. The result is well known: humiliation, massive bloodshed and, eventually, enforced retreat. Returning to Western Europe, Napoleon's depleted and demoralized troops encountered the allied forces of Prussia, Russia and Austria at Leipzig on October 18, 1813; Wagner was then five months old. In what has since come to be known as 'The Battle of the Nations' the allies were victorious, but only with horrifying losses on both sides. It is estimated that around 100,000 men were left dead or dying on the battlefields around the city.

As the future great composer proceeded through infancy, the grand historical drama moved rapidly to its climax. Exiled to the Mediterranean island of Elba in 1814, Napoleon staged a dramatic return the following year, only to suffer his final defeat in June 1815 just outside the Belgian village of Waterloo.

Meanwhile, at the Congress of Vienna (1814–15), decisions were taken that would shape the destiny of Wagner's homeland for generations to come. Representatives of all the major European powers met to re-establish order and redraw national boundaries in the wake of the Napoleonic upheaval. Some of those overwhelmingly conservative diplomats were motivated by a desire to put the clock back, and to banish memories of the French Revolution from the collective consciousness. There was to be no more talk of republicanism, of extending democracy or the 'Rights of Man'. But as so often, repression bred resistance: at first only in the minds of the few, but eventually in bloody reality. Wagner himself would be caught up in that spirit of resistance – and he was to be no mere armchair revolutionary.

Despite the crushing of Napoleon, and the subsequent attempts to purge Europe of his ideas, the world he left behind had been transformed forever. It was as a member of a newly empowered middle class that the young Wagner found his social bearing and his ideals – the very class whose liberal intellectuals had made such a major contribution to the early stages of the French Revolution. While rule in the German-speaking lands was to remain reactionary for some while after the resolutions of Vienna, within this newly mapped Europe there were powerful new forces to be contended with. If French Revolutionary ideas had been suppressed (for the moment), the consequences of the Industrial Revolution needed to be accommodated: in particular mass production, redistribution of wealth and the attendant rise of the educated and enriched bourgeoisie. Wagner would eventually learn – after years of poverty, obscurity and even political exile – to turn the

> It was as a member of a newly empowered middle class that the young Wagner found his social bearing and his ideals – the very class whose liberal intellectuals had made such a major contribution to the early stages of the French Revolution.

public attitudes and secret desires of this rising class to his own advantage. The composer's feeling for the spirit of his age, and his ability to tap directly into certain aspects of it, are two of the more interesting facets of his many-sided genius.

Artistic Ancestry

Baptized 'Wilhelm Richard', Wagner was the youngest of nine children born to Friedrich Wagner, a police actuary and later police chief, and his wife Johanna (Rosine), *née* Pätz. The infant Richard had scant time to get to know his father: Friedrich died on November 23, 1813, a victim of the typhus epidemic that swept through the city after the Battle of Leipzig. Things might have become very hard indeed for Johanna Wagner, with no source of income and a large family to look after. Fortunately she married the actor, painter and poet Ludwig Geyer on August 28, 1814, after which the new family moved to the Saxon capital Dresden, where Geyer had been engaged by the Court Theatre.

> The composer's feeling for the spirit of his age, and his ability to tap directly into certain aspects of it, are two of the more interesting facets of his many-sided genius.

There has been much speculation about the length of time that Johanna and Geyer had been intimate, and consequently about the paternity of young Richard. In later years Wagner oscillated between believing that Geyer was his father and emphatically rejecting the idea, though of one thing he seems to have been quite sure. 'My mother loved him – they were kindred spirits,' he remarked. As an actor and enthusiast for the theatre, Geyer must have been tolerant of its notoriously 'Bohemian' morals, so illicit liaisons may well have been par for the course. They certainly were for Friedrich Wagner, who was a close friend of Geyer; jokes about Friedrich's partiality for actresses were part of Wagner family lore.

Wagner's musical inheritance was a strong one either way. Friedrich was descended from a two-century-long line of Saxon schoolmasters and Kantors (the German term for the director of music at a Protestant church). Geyer too came from a musical family, which dated back to Benjamin Geyer, organist at the Andreaskirche in Eisleben in 1700. Those who like to trace the genetic ancestry of genius have made much of the fact that, if Geyer was Wagner's father, Richard also had the theatre in his blood. Whatever the case, Geyer's presence meant that Wagner was steeped in the theatrical milieu from his earliest years. As a boy he was encouraged to take part: there is a story of him appearing on the stage as an angel, with wings strapped to his back, struggling to maintain a graceful pose. This early immersion in the theatre – in its backstage activities as well as the business on the stage – was a major formative influence. It helps to explain the older Wagner's extraordinary feeling for the element of spectacle in his operas and music dramas as well as the unusual practicality he showed in making his visions work, no matter how audacious the thinking behind them. It is also possible that in building his own 'Festival Theatre' at Bayreuth, Wagner was in a sense recreating something of his childhood world, or at least that aspect of his early life that he had found least problematic. In his autobiography, *Mein Leben* (*My Life*), Wagner says that, as a youth, he quickly realized 'the importance the theatrical had assumed in [his] mind in comparison with the ordinary bourgeois life'.

Paternity and Prejudice

The question mark over Wagner's parentage acquired extra significance in the years following Wagner's death – and this brings us on to what is probably the most difficult aspect of Wagner and his music: his anti-Semitism. A rumor as to Wagner's possible Jewish ancestry appears to have spread following the publication of Friedrich Nietzsche's incisively polemical *Der Fall Wagner* (*The Case of Wagner*, 1888). Nietzsche had been a passionate admirer of Wagner in his twenties, and for a while had been a regular and very welcome guest at the Wagner home. It seems that Wagner made certain remarks to Nietzsche about the matter of his paternity, which Nietzsche later picked up and ran with energetically. In a famously waspish footnote to *Der Fall Wagner*, Nietzsche asks: 'Was Wagner a German at all? There are some reasons for this question... His father was an actor by the name of Geyer. A Geyer is almost an Adler.' In German *Geyer* means 'vulture', while *Adler* means 'eagle' – emblem of German rule since the first Habsburg emperors. The inference that some readers appear to have drawn is that Geyer was a Jewish name. Although there is no evidence that Geyer had any Jewish blood at all, the thought that music's most notorious anti-Semite might have been half-Jewish has appealed to a variety of people, and for a variety of reasons.

There is also no evidence that Wagner even hinted to Nietzsche that he suspected himself to have Jewish blood; but the fact that the rumor proved so tenacious confirms the complexity of many issues surrounding Wagner's character. Might it be that Wagner saw something of himself in the grotesque anti-Semitic caricatures that were all too common in his homeland (and elsewhere) by the middle of the nineteenth century? As a child Wagner was sickly, and at first there were doubts that he would survive. It is possible that this sickliness affected his physical development: he remained small, pale and thin with an abnormally large head (especially across the

> Might it be that Wagner saw something of himself in the grotesque anti-Semitic caricatures that were all too common in his homeland (and elsewhere) by the middle of the nineteenth century?

forehead). His appearance made him highly self-conscious, and something of that appalled self-awareness may have found its way into his characterizations of the villainous dwarves Alberich and Mime in his huge operatic tetralogy **Der Ring des Nibelungen** ('The Ring of the Nibelungs'). Mime in particular is described in Wagner's original stage directions as 'small and bent, somewhat deformed and hobbling, his head is abnormally large'. Given the adult Wagner's overt racism, some critics have interpreted Alberich and Mime as fairly typical nineteenth-century anti-Semitic caricatures – an interpretation which has some force, except that it ignores Wagner's later admission that he felt sorry for Alberich in particular, and disturbed by his humiliation at the hands of the gods. Still, the German social philosopher Theodor Adorno surely comes close to the mark in his *Versuch über Wagner* (*In Search of Wagner*, 1952). Paraphrasing his colleague Walter Benjamin, Adorno finds expressions of disgust towards something to be symptomatic of 'the fear of being thought to be the same as that which is found disgusting'.

This is not to excuse Wagner's racist beliefs. Nevertheless, if we are to identify that which is good in his art and thus rescue it from the more unpleasant aspects of his ideology, then it is important that he is seen as a human being – if a very flawed one – and not as a monster.

CD 1 track 7–11
CD 2 track 8–10

www.naxosbooks.com

Website

www.naxosbooks.com

A Disturbed Imagination

In accounts of his early childhood there are other interesting indications of the kind of man Wagner was to become. Despite Geyer's benign protective presence (he clearly cared for young Richard as though he were his own), there were signs of an intense, disturbed imagination. The traumas of war and the death of his father when Wagner was a baby could well have been contributory factors. In *Mein Leben* Wagner tells how every night he would wake screaming from terrible dreams. His siblings refused to sleep near him and he was banished to a room at the end of the family apartment, where he felt even more isolated and frightened. The visceral terror evoked by the music he provided for the dragon in *Der Ring des Nibelungen* is surely rooted in similar dark imaginings. Along with these he seems quickly to have developed a sense of the world as an alien and fearful place. In addition, the demands on Johanna Wagner in bringing up a large family almost certainly meant that she had little time or maternal tenderness to spend on her troubled youngest child: that, at least, was Wagner's explanation. He did not remember her as a very comforting or affectionate presence, though he retained strong feelings of loyalty and devotion to her. All of this helps to explain why for much of his life Wagner yearned for someone – preferably a female someone – to rescue him from his sense of dreadful loneliness. Something of that frightened longing must have found its way into the haunted monologues of the accursed Dutchman in *Der Fliegende Holländer* ('The Flying Dutchman'), who hopes against hope for the redeeming love of a good woman – and perhaps also into the desperation of the sick Tristan, aching for the return of the woman he loves.

For much of his life Wagner yearned for someone – preferably a female someone – to rescue him from his sense of dreadful loneliness.

Among his peers, young Wagner could be arrogant and sharp-tongued. He also showed a flair for getting into confrontations, but in spite of his impressive physical agility and strength (for someone of small stature) he drew back from any impulse to inflict physical pain. Although there is violence in Wagner's operas, it is rarely glorified, and in the everyday world he often found it profoundly unsettling. Suffering in animals caused him particular distress: there are stories of his rescuing puppies from drowning and having to be held back from rushing in when he saw a butcher slaughtering an ox. It has become a truism to assert that those who care excessively for animals are often lacking in sympathy for their fellow beings. Evidence for that in Wagner's adult life can readily be produced; and yet there are also accounts of his being horrified by public executions and stories of the treatment of prisoners. Turn to the music and it is hard to resist the impression that Wagner was capable of great compassion for human suffering – as is indicated by the portrayals of the Dutchman and Tristan, and still more the incurably wounded Amfortas in *Parsifal*.

At the age of seven, Wagner was taken into the care of a Lutheran Pastor, Christian Wetzel, who lived just outside Dresden in the village of Possendorf. As with Geyer, Wetzel's influence seems to have been largely benevolent, which could partly explain why, despite later revolutionary, republican leanings, Wagner never entirely rejected Christianity. Though hostile to church authority and dogmatism, he returned again and again in his work to Christian imagery. He retained a thoroughly Protestant suspicion of Papal authority (witness the description of the Pope's harsh inflexibility in *Tannhäuser*), and in later years his mistrust of the Jesuits verged on the paranoiac. Yet the imagery and emotion associated with the Mass in *Parsifal* is overwhelmingly positive. The communion rite's ritual and symbolism would have appealed to Wagner's theatrical instincts, but that his fascination went deeper than mere display is beyond doubt.

Musician or Poet?

Around the time that he entered Wetzel's household, Wagner had his first piano lessons. As yet, though, there were no signs of precocious musical talent. When the eight-year-old boy was called urgently back to Dresden, where Geyer was on his deathbed, he was asked to play something on the piano, and Geyer is said to have remarked to Johanna, 'You don't suppose he might be musical?' Some Wagnerians have seen this anecdote as proof that there was nothing artificially 'cultivated' about Wagner's genius – that it developed according to its own laws, as a force of nature. But it is also possible that Geyer was being genuinely perceptive: he had already made it clear that he thought young Richard had potential. In *Mein Leben* Wagner put an ironic spin on his dying stepfather's words, but this may well have been a misrepresentation.

When Wagner entered the Dresden Kreuzschule ('School of the Cross') in 1822, he did so as 'Richard Geyer', though this is probably no more than a reflection of the conventions of nineteenth-century middle-class respectability. At school Wagner's progress was erratic; but he quickly developed a passion for Ancient Greek literature and history, especially its heroic mythological subjects. Young as he was, Wagner may have sensed a degree of contemporary relevance here. For the rising Romantic generation Greek art had taken on new significance: no longer held up as the standard for formal 'classical' rules, but as an ideal of otherworldly, transcendent beauty – a kind of Utopia of the mind for those disillusioned with the promises of the French Revolution. Keats's famous *Ode on a Grecian Urn*, written in 1819, has its central image of the vase as the 'still unravished bride of quietness'. That same year Schubert had composed his song 'Die Götter Griechenlands' ('The Gods of Greece'), with its poignant, nostalgic opening cry, 'Schöne Welt, wo bist du?' ('Beautiful world, where are you?'). It was in the same spirit that Schumann later praised Mozart's Symphony No. 40 for its 'Grecian lightness and grace'. Wagner's researches into

At school Wagner's progress was erratic; but he quickly developed a passion for Ancient Greek literature and history, especially its heroic mythological subjects.

the literature of Ancient Greece would eventually take him far beyond this increasingly popular and increasingly sentimental idealism. For the moment, though, he was happy to comply with his school's conception of good classical versifying. When a pupil suddenly dropped dead in class, the school suggested that fellow pupils submit commemorative poems. To the delight of his mother, Wagner's eulogy was singled out as the best. The boy's destiny was clear: he was to become a poet.

In 1826, when Wagner was thirteen, his eldest sister Rosalie was offered work as an actress at a Prague theatre. As she was now the chief breadwinner, the family moved with her, but Wagner remained in Dresden. During a school trip to Leipzig the following year he met his uncle Adolf Wagner, a respected scholar whose work had been praised by the great Goethe. Adolf encouraged his nephew's intellectual pursuits, and gave him a number of books that had belonged to Ludwig Geyer. Thus the young Wagner began to build what would eventually be an impressive library.

His mother and two of his sisters returned from Prague to Leipzig, which enabled Wagner to leave Dresden and join them, and thus spend more time with his uncle. It may be a sign of Uncle Adolf's influence that about this time the young Richard readopted the surname Wagner. In January 1828 he entered the Nicolaischule (St. Nicholas School) in Leipzig, but by this time his private creative agenda was beginning to interfere seriously with his studies. Obsessed with the theatre, he wrote a tragedy called *Leubald*, full of ghosts, madness and murder. Wagner may again have been showing an awareness of the artistic fashions of his day: such subject matter is the very life-blood of 'gothic' literature, which was at its height of popularity in the early decades of the nineteenth century. The school authorities were not impressed, however,

> Obsessed with the theatre, he wrote a tragedy called *Leubald*, full of ghosts, madness and murder.

nor was his mother. Wagner was rebuked for wasting both time and talent.

Far from feeling chastened, Wagner began to nurture another private creative obsession. After hearing some of Beethoven's symphonies, as well as Carl Maria von Weber's sensational new opera *Der Freischütz* (*The Free-Shooter*), he made up his mind to apply himself to music. Wagner got hold of a copy of a book by the widely influential musical pedagogue Johann Bernhard Logier, *Thorough-bass* (the old term for harmonic theory). He also began harmony lessons – at first in secret – with the musical director Christian Gottlieb Müller. That Wagner dedicated himself to studying harmony at an early age is significant because it was precisely in this field that he was to achieve far-reaching innovations. As with so many of the great musical mold-breakers, rejecting the rules came only after mastering them. Unfortunately, and also rather characteristically, Wagner does not appear to have reckoned with the cost involved in private study. His debts mounted, and the secret came out, again to his mother's horror.

> That Wagner dedicated himself to studying harmony at an early age is significant because it was precisely in this field that he was to achieve far-reaching innovations.

First Compositions

Undaunted by all this disapproval, Wagner made his first attempts at composition. From 1829 date two piano sonatas and a string quartet – all of which, sadly, are lost. Also in that year Wagner heard Beethoven's opera *Fidelio* for the first time, with the famous soprano Wilhelmine Schröder-Devrient in the role of Leonore. The music bowled him over, and the story of political repression and a prisoner rescued by his heroic, loving wife left a lasting impression. It seems the die was now cast. At Easter the following year, the sixteen-year-old Wagner left the Nicolaischule and began taking violin lessons. He also got hold of a score of Beethoven's Ninth Symphony and made a piano transcription. This monumental, complex work with its ferociously difficult choral finale may be regarded as one of the greatest of artistic treasures today, but in the early nineteenth century many saw it as an aberration on Beethoven's part, and it was rarely performed even passably well. Wagner, however, seems to have sensed something of immense personal significance in the way that Beethoven strove to bridge the gap between purely orchestral symphonic music and a sung text.

More compositions followed – and now Wagner tried his hand at orchestral writing. Three overtures date from 1830, including what is now referred to as the 'Drumbeat' Overture– which, with typical ostentation, Wagner intended to present to the world in several different colors of ink (an ambition slightly dented by his inability to find any green). He did manage to find a conductor, and Heinrich Dorn, Kapellmeister at the Leipzig Court Theatre, directed a performance in December. It was a spectacular failure. The main problem appears to have been Wagner's bizarre idea of making every fifth bar silent except for a *fortissimo* thud from the timpani on the second beat. At first mystified, the audience soon fell about laughing and Wagner fled the hall in shame.

Wagner, however, seems to have sensed something of immense personal significance in the way that Beethoven strove to bridge the gap between purely orchestral symphonic music and a sung text.

More application was clearly needed. In February 1831 Wagner enrolled at Leipzig University with the intention of studying music, though it was not until the following year that he found a teacher who suited him. Christian Theodor Weinlig was Kantor at the Thomaskirche – the post held by J.S. Bach in the previous century. Despite the recent misadventure of the 'Drumbeat' Overture, Weinlig recognized Wagner's talent and encouraged it, setting him extensive and demanding composition exercises. In later years Wagner was inclined to play down the importance of Weinlig's teaching, partly, no doubt, for reasons of personal vanity. But creative people are often inclined to undervalue the influence of their teachers, something that Wagner's future friend Nietzsche understood only too well. At one point in Nietzsche's philosophical poem *Also Sprach Zarathustra* (*Thus Spake Zarathustra*) his prophet–hero tells his disciples: 'I will not believe you have truly learned from me until you deny I taught you anything.'

Youthful Idealism

The first clear signs of Wagner the political activist also emerge at around this time – though as with composing, his initial efforts have a more than slightly comic tinge. In July 1830, resentment against the reactionary regime of the French King Charles X finally boiled over into revolution. The explosion had its echoes elsewhere, including Leipzig, where there were student marches and street fights. At one point Wagner found himself caught up in the storming of a brothel – a symbol of the old repressive order for many liberal activists. The next morning he woke up with a terrible hangover, a strip of red curtain beside him as a trophy of the previous night's spoils, and little memory as to what had actually happened. But the students' notion of freedom had its limits. When the working classes joined in the disturbances, and there began to be talk of the confiscation of property and the total abolition of social rank, the students began to side with the authorities, and Wagner went along with them. At this stage, it seems, revolutionary talk was still more of an undergraduate posture than a reflection of a genuinely held, thought-through ideology.

Weinlig pronounced Wagner's musical studies complete in 1832, and in this year another orchestral work, the Symphony in C, was performed. Though obviously indebted to Beethoven and Mozart, it was far more successful than the unfortunate 'Drumbeat' Overture, and a second performance was given at Leipzig's famous concert hall, the Gewandhaus, in January 1833. Having finished his studies, Wagner spent some time near Prague on the estate of Count Pachta, who had been sufficiently impressed with the young man to invite him to stay. There Wagner fell violently in love with one of the Count's daughters, the dark-haired Jenny. In years to come Wagner would enjoy a number of amorous conquests, but at this stage he was, by his own admission, a disastrous suitor. In *Mein Leben* Wagner chides his younger self for a 'passion for intimacy, the mania for instructing, the zeal for converting' (not that the older Wagner was in any position to judge). At the time, in a letter to his new friend, the helpfully wealthy Theodor Apel, Wagner shows that he was capable of realistic self-appraisal even when young: 'My idealizing vision saw in her everything it desired to see, and that was the cause of my misfortune!' It is debatable as to whether Wagner ever rose above that 'idealizing vision' when it came to potential lovers.

In years to come Wagner would enjoy a number of amorous conquests, but at this stage he was, by his own admission, a disastrous suitor.

Also in 1832 Wagner wrote the libretto for an opera, *Die Hochzeit* (*The Wedding*). Some of the music was composed early the following year, but when Wagner showed what he had written of this 'nocturnal piece of the darkest hue' to his sister Rosalie, she urged him to destroy it. Wagner complied, but only after he had put some of the music before his teacher. Weinlig was impressed by one of the musical numbers, a septet, and he praised Wagner's vocal writing – a timely, encouraging judgement.

A Devouring Flame

At this stage Wagner was still pursuing a bohemian drifter's lifestyle, carousing with students and actors, and developing an alarming taste for gambling. There is a story that in one particularly heavy session he even staked his mother's pension – fortunately on that occasion he won. Frank confession and eventual forgiveness followed, but his mother and sister Rosalie made no secret of their anxiety about his activities. From this period must stem something of the mature Wagner's contempt for money, and for capitalist money-makers, expressed so powerfully in the symbol of the accursed golden ring that brings destruction on its owners in *Das Rheingold* (*The Rhinegold*) and *Götterdämmerung* (*Twilight of the Gods*), the first and last of the *Ring* tetralogy. There was nothing hypocritical about the older Wagner's condemnation of financial greed; but while he disdained money and those who strove for it he developed a lasting taste for the luxuries it could buy, and counting the cost never came easily to him. Some of this may have been compensation for the sense of deprivation he admitted to feeling as a child; but it was to get him into trouble over and over again. As Wagner's biographer Ernest Newman put it: 'The full extent of his borrowings and his debts, even at this early period in his life, will never be known; but one feels a sort of terror at the hints as to the total of them that are given here and there in *Mein Leben* and his letters.'

A series of letters written to Theodor Apel in 1835 give some sense of the turmoil Wagner found himself in repeatedly as a result of his debts. They swing from abject breast-beating through self-justification to passionate expressions of repentance – all conveyed in the most colorful, theatrical language:

> Wagner was still pursuing a bohemian drifter's lifestyle, carousing with students and actors, and developing an alarming taste for gambling.

I have sinned – yet not so! Does a man sin when he is mad? I have fallen out with my family, and must regard our relations as at an end...

Dear friend, I was not wicked, I was mad: that is the only explanation I can find for my behavior...

I have formed the conviction that money is as much a living force as the human society in which we exist. I was mad, I repeat, for I did not understand either myself or my relationship to the world. I knew that I had no strong foothold or support, yet I acted like one insane, lived beyond my means in every respect, with the ignorance and inexperience of a man who has never had any solid entitlement to money; no one, not even a wealthy man, throws money away as I did. The result is a whirlpool of confusion and misery, the tangled consequences of which I cannot contemplate without dismay...

And then come the inevitable pleas for help:

I cannot go back... until I have removed the burden of a debt of 400 talers. So here I stand – I am forsaken by and cut off from everyone: everyone on whom I might otherwise be able to count, on top which is the most painful anxiety for my mother. She can give me nothing. You are the only one left to whom I can turn...

Gifts of money bring profuse gratitude and resolutions to do better. For a week or two all seems well: Wagner is writing energetically and delighted with what he is producing. Then the plaint is resumed again: 'Dearest friend, I must have money if I am not to go mad...'

Unattractive as all this may be, in the background to this story there remains a paradox. Despite his all-too-glaring faults, Wagner never had any difficulty in making – and sometimes keeping – good friends. Apel, for one, evidently enjoyed his company and remained on good terms with him for several years, despite Wagner's many subsequent changes of address, and despite those gut-churning continual requests for money.

However infuriating Wagner may have been to those who loved him, love him they did. His sister Rosalie, for instance, remained close to him despite all the trials he put her through. With others, love would yield to open veneration. Then there are those men who recognized something of value in the young Wagner and tried to help him: Ludwig Geyer, Adolf Wagner, Heinrich Dorn, Christian Theodor Weinlig. Certainly Wagner could be a charmer when he wanted to be. He had great charisma, enhanced by a kind of sensual allure that had nothing to do with conventional physical beauty. But even that does not account for the long and patient devotion that many showed both to him and to his art. Perhaps only those who knew Wagner could explain how 'this devouring flame of a man', as he was described by Newman, was able to inspire such loyalty, admiration, even affection; but with the music it is another matter.

> However infuriating Wagner may have been to those who loved him, love him they did.

Chapter 2
The Road to Paris

The Road to Paris

Wagner's first professional breakthrough came in January 1833 – his twentieth year. His brother Albert, who was working at the theatre in Würzburg, found Wagner a job there as chorus master. This was a wonderful learning opportunity: Wagner's imaginative chorus writing in *Der Fliegende Holländer*, even more impressive in *Parsifal*, clearly owes something to this early hands-on experience. Having to coach the chorus for Weber's *Der Freischütz* and Beethoven's *Fidelio* enriched Wagner's understanding of works that had already become important to him. There were formative encounters with other influential Romantic operas, among them Heinrich Marschner's *Der Vampyr* (*The Vampire*) and Giacomo Meyerbeer's *Robert le Diable* (*Robert the Devil*); the titles give enough hint of their content, which the young Wagner, with his taste for the supernatural, would have found very agreeable. At his brother's instigation he wrote a new, more vocally acrobatic ending for one of the arias in *Der Vampyr*. Albert was delighted, and it was performed, apparently with some success.

Meanwhile Wagner was surveying material for an opera of his own. He looked at a libretto by the radical young writer Heinrich Laube, but although it impressed him he drew the conclusion that he could do just as good a job himself. His confidence was further boosted by two short but enjoyable love affairs, one with a soprano from the chorus who came to Wagner for singing lessons. The composer then came across a story by the Italian fabulist Carlo Gozzi, *La Donna Serpente* (*The Snake Woman*); this he made the basis of his first complete opera, *Die Feen* (*The Fairies*).

Die Feen was conceived very much in the Weber–Marschner supernatural mode, from which an increasingly distinctive German Romantic style of opera composition was already emerging. This had its roots partly in eighteenth-century *Singspiel* (literally 'sung play'), which was originally a kind of opera in German with relatively simple musical numbers alongside spoken dialogue, but whose musical language increased in complexity and dramatic fluidity, culminating in Mozart's *Die Zauberflöte* (*The Magic Flute*, 1791). Beethoven's *Fidelio* had shown how the musical contribution – including the role of the orchestral overture – could be expanded, and the plots be made to incorporate heroic and political themes. Then Weber's *Der Freischütz* had moved still further towards German Romantic nationalism by introducing folkloric elements into both the storylines and the musical style – especially in the vocal writing. Weber also greatly enriched the musical representation of nature: for example, the forest imagery in *Freischütz* (hunting horns; string tremolos representing mystery, rustling foliage and so on). It was also noticeable that, with Weber in particular, the harmonic language of German Romantic opera was becoming more chromatic, more intensely expressive. While the Italians, and to a certain extent the French, relied on the power of melody to convey emotions, the Germans were turning more towards expressive harmony. All this was to be of huge formative significance for the young Wagner.

Website

www.naxosbooks.com

> While the Italians, and to a certain extent the French, relied on the power of melody to convey emotions, the Germans were turning more towards expressive harmony. All this was to be of huge formative significance for the young Wagner.

Young Germany

On a visit to Leipzig in 1834 Wagner met Heinrich Laube, whose libretto Wagner had looked at the previous year, and an influential friendship began. Laube's positive review of Wagner's Symphony in C was a good start, but Wagner quickly became impressed by his political views as well as the passion with which he argued them. That some of Laube's work had actually been banned made him even more exciting. Laube was a leading figure in the radical movement known as 'Young Germany', which was generally republican, democratic, and often nationalistic in view. It is important to stress that in the early nineteenth century nationalism was by no means the right-wing, authoritarian phenomenon it so often appears to be today (even though some young radicals were inclined towards the notion of a 'benevolent dictatorship'). In those times the idea of a nation – a group of people defined in terms of culture and ancestry – as an entity in its own right, independent of its ruler, was highly subversive. For the typical conservative, the monarch was a God-given fact, and his people were his subjects. When the French King Louis XIV made the famous pronouncement 'L'État c'est moi' ('I am the State') he was simply articulating what many took for granted in the seventeenth and eighteenth centuries. So the notion that a people, or even its cultural elite, might be able to define its own political destiny was seen as deeply threatening by the powers established in the wake of the Vienna Congress.

However nationalistic the Young Germans may have been, many of them still felt they had much to learn from other nations: the revolutionary French, for instance, or the Italians with their 'natural' expressivity, and their very Mediterranean understanding of the importance of love between the sexes. Hearing Wilhelmine Schröder-Devrient in Bellini's opera

I Capuleti e i Montecchi strengthened Wagner's appreciation of Italian sensibilities in both respects. Shakespeare's *Romeo and Juliet* (ultimately derived from the same tragic renaissance love story as *I Capuleti e i Montecchi*) came to be seen as a key text by many German Romantics. Here was an intensely poetic portrayal of sexual love as a force that can change society: in this case bringing about the reconciliation of two warring families. For the Young Germans, love was exalted to the status of a revolutionary force – as Karl Marx observed with contempt some years later. For Wagner, with his self-confessed idealizing tendency when it came to erotic love, this was a spark to dry tinder. The notion of Eros as not only personally redeeming but socially transforming survived for quite a while, though Wagner's attitude towards sexual love was to grow increasingly complex, especially after his life-changing encounter with the philosophy of Schopenhauer two decades later.

Wagner expressed his new-found Young German enthusiasm in an article entitled 'Die Deutsche Oper' ('German Opera'), which Laube published in his own journal in June 1834. This was to be the first of many published essays which Wagner has left to posterity. Some of them give evidence of a profound and highly original thinker; others, like the notorious 'Das Judenthum in der Musik' ('Jewishness in Music'), show what a graceless bigot he could be. As evidence of the development of his innovatory ideas Wagner's writings can be very illuminating, but they are rarely easy to read. This is partly because his literary style tends to tip over into the unfocused intoxication with language that makes the writings of the pioneering German philosopher of history, Georg Wilhelm Friedrich Hegel, so difficult to read. It also mars the productions of so many of Hegel's admirers in the first half of the nineteenth century – a period memorably

As evidence of the development of his innovatory ideas Wagner's writings can be very illuminating, but they are rarely easy to read.

25

summed up by one modern writer as 'Philosophy's wild years'. Though again Wagner was capable of shafts of self-awareness: on one occasion, reading aloud from a philosophical work that fired his enthusiasm, Wagner found himself challenged by a friend – what did it all mean? Wagner paused for a moment, then burst out laughing, adding, 'You know, I haven't a clue!'

In June 1834 Wagner enjoyed a walking tour in Bohemia with his friend Theodor Apel, who had aspirations to be a romantic poet. The two men attempted to live as hedonistic, 'Mediterranean' a life as possible, with plenty of robust intellectual discussion for good measure. Bohemia's forests were the setting for *Der Freischütz*, as Wagner would have been well aware. Under the influence of the Romantics, the forest was becoming as potent a symbol for Germans as the sea has been for English writers, painters and composers. Consider how many of the formative, magical encounters in the fairy tales of the Brothers Grimm take place in forests. It was to be in a similar magical woodland setting that Wagner's hero Siegfried would find his identity, his destiny and his ideal love, to the accompaniment of some of Wagner's most atmospheric tone-painting. Under the influence of this holiday, Wagner began to sketch out his second opera, **Das Liebesverbot** (*The Ban on Love*), which was based on Shakespeare's *Measure for Measure* but with the setting transferred from Vienna to a Mediterranean island.

> On one occasion, reading aloud from a philosophical work that fired his enthusiasm, Wagner found himself challenged by a friend – what did it all mean? Wagner paused for a moment, then burst out laughing, adding, 'You know, I haven't a clue!'

Website

www.naxosbooks.com

As in Shakespeare's play, love – here specifically sexual love – triumphs over harsh authoritarianism by revealing that the tyrant, Friedrich, is as governed by desire as are those whom he tries to repress. Wagner deliberately turned away from German operatic models towards those of Italy, particularly, it seems, Donizetti. This can be heard in the score's relative lightness of touch, its quick-moving comedy and, above all else, its celebration of melody. This leaning towards Italian models and general ideals was clearly an important detour for Wagner, possibly enriching his musical language more than if he had simply carried on where *Die Feen* left off. Still, there remains something fatally heavy about it all – the sparkle of the best Donizetti is lacking – and *Das Liebesverbot* has never been popular.

Minna

On returning from his holiday, Wagner discovered that he had been offered the job of musical director in Heinrich Bethmann's theatre company; it was based in Magdeburg, but regularly undertook extensive tours during the summer months. Wagner hastened to meet up with the company, where it was announced to him that he was expected to prepare a performance of Mozart's *Don Giovanni* by the weekend. He refused point blank. But then he encountered one of the company's leading actresses, Wilhelmine ('Minna') Planer, and instantly changed his mind. Physically attractive, Minna also possessed a mixture of openness and dignified poise that appealed strongly to Wagner. *Don Giovanni* went ahead after all. This was Wagner's debut as a conductor and it was very well received.

He was expected to prepare a performance of Mozart's *Don Giovanni* by the weekend. He refused point blank. But then he encountered one of the company's leading actresses, and instantly changed his mind.

On a return visit to Leipzig in 1835, Wagner discovered how dangerous it was to be identified publicly with the Young Germans. The authorities had already begun a crackdown on dissident intellectuals, and now Laube was arrested and sent to prison. Wagner did not desert his friend: indeed, he tried to help him to escape when the arrest warrant was issued. He was shocked by the experience, however, and hurried back to the

Bethmann troupe, and to Minna. At first she played hard to get – given Wagner's 'idealizing' nature, and his tendency to desire the unattainable, this could have been shrewd gamesmanship on her part. But when Wagner was struck down with one of his periodic skin complaints (almost certainly psychosomatic) she nursed him tenderly. The foundations of an enduring, if stormy, relationship were laid. When Minna left in November 1835 to work in Berlin he bombarded her with passionate love letters. No sooner had she gone than she received the following:

> *Minna, my state of mind cannot be described. You are gone, and my heart is broken. I sit here barely in control of myself, weeping and sobbing like a child.*

She was back less than two weeks later.

The Composer Takes the Stage

Wagner now began to use his success with Bethmann's company to his own advantage. In 1835 he arranged a performance of Apel's play *Columbus*, for which he provided incidental music. In a major coup he persuaded Schröder-Devrient to sing under his baton, though the concerts were disastrous financially and musically – partly because Wagner insisted on a hugely expanded orchestra for Beethoven's 'Battle Symphony', with real cannons for added effect. The acoustic could not cope with it; neither could the audience, and the hall emptied.

At the end of March, however, Wagner managed to secure a performance of his newly completed *Das Liebesverbot* – though not before the police authorities succeeded in getting the opera's inflammatory title changed to the more innocuous *Die Novize von Palermo* ('The Novice of Palermo'). It failed, and then to cap it all, Bethmann's company went bankrupt. Wagner was without a position again.

Then Minna was offered another acting job, this time in the Baltic port of Königsberg (now Kaliningrad). This was considerably further away than Berlin, but she promised to try to secure a position for Wagner while she was there. Impatient with both her absence and apparent lack of success, Wagner followed soon after; but the post of musical director at the theatre was not yet vacant. Wagner decided to bide his time. While he was waiting, he and Minna were married in November, despite growing tensions in their relationship. Wagner wanted a wife who would be loyal to him, his art, and his ideals, but Minna had little time for politics and philosophy, and she seems from the first to have regarded theirs as an 'open' relationship. The day before the wedding, the priest opened his door to find the couple rowing furiously on his doorstep. But all three saw the funny side of this, and the marriage went ahead.

Minna Planer (1809–1866), Wagner's first wife

At last, on April 1, 1837, Wagner was delighted to receive an invitation to become musical director at the Königsberg Theatre. He was rather less delighted with what he found there. The theatre was nearly bankrupt, employees were expected to work for little or no pay, and morale was abysmal. Then, suddenly, Minna took up with a merchant called Dietrich. Financial hardship must have been partly to blame. Wagner raced off in furious pursuit of her seducer but he had vanished, as Wagner noted pithily in his diary: 'Whips, pistols, D. already gone.' He then tracked Minna down to her parents' house in Dresden. She had no intention of going back to Königsberg and poverty, but she did eventually join

Wagner in an apartment he had found just outside Dresden. There he found solace, as he often did, in reading. This time it was Edward Bulwer-Lytton's latest historical novel, *Rienzi, the Last of the Roman Tribunes*. Wagner was gripped, and the idea for another opera was born.

At this seeming low point in his professional career, deliverance came, again from the north. Wagner's efforts to attain a post at Riga, up the coast from Königsberg, had paid off. This meant more professional openings for him, and a proper salary. Wagner left on his own, and arrived in Riga on August 21. The conditions he found there were not encouraging, but when he received a 'truly moving' letter from Minna, in which she confessed her guilt and begged forgiveness, he was magnanimous – to the point of shouldering some of the blame – and invited her to join him in Riga. She set off soon afterwards, bringing her younger sister Amalie, whom Wagner had managed to engage as prima donna in the theatre company. He was now hard at work on the score for *Rienzi*, but he still had time to organize – in addition to his theatre duties – a series of six concerts. In these he managed to include symphonies by Beethoven (though still not the hugely demanding Ninth), Mozart's Symphony No. 40, and overtures by Weber and Mendelssohn. In the midst of this came the very sad news that Wagner's sister Rosalie had died. Despite her criticism of his student dissipations and her condemnation of his first operatic effort *Die Hochzeit*, Rosalie had always been Wagner's favorite.

The Flight from Riga

Wagner's stay at Riga lasted until March 1839. He might have put up with the frustrations of provincial musical life for longer, but a clever piece of power-play by the theatre's former director, Karl von Holtei, made it impossible for Wagner's contract to be renewed, even though the new director, Josef Hoffmann, was very much on his side. There was only one real possibility now: he must go to Paris, operatic capital of the world, and make his fortune. Surely there his *Rienzi* would find the appreciation it deserved. He sent letters to the opera composer Giacomo Meyerbeer – then at the pinnacle of his reputation in Paris – and to the equally successful librettist Eugène Scribe, and began to plan his escape from Riga. It would have to be secret: the Wagners' debts had reached such a level that their passports had been confiscated. A loyal friend, Abraham Möller, smuggled them across the frontier, from where they could make their way to an East Prussian port, and then get themselves on board a boat.

It was a good plan, but things began going wrong almost immediately. For a start, Wagner's enormous Newfoundland, Robber, refused to be parted from him and followed the couple across the border. It is fortunate that Newfoundlands are not particularly vocal dogs, or Robber might have given them away to the guards.

Safely across the Prussian border, the Wagners met up with Möller again. Now the Wagners plus dog were squeezed into a rickety cart, which wobbled its way along primitive roads, finally overturning in a farmyard. Minna was badly hurt, and Wagner was pitched into a dungheap. A miserable night in a peasant hut followed, after which they somehow managed to get to the port of Pillau (now Baltiysk). There they furtively boarded a schooner called *Thetis* (Robber had to be winched over the side) and hid below deck to avoid the customs officers. In this they were successful; but during their journey a terrible storm blew up, and Wagner and Minna were prostrate with fear and seasickness.

Eventually the *Thetis* was forced to seek harbor in the Norwegian fishing village of Sandviken. Here, according to *Mein Leben*, inspiration suddenly came: 'one of the most wonderful impressions of my life,' Wagner called it. Deeply struck by the rocky coastal scenery as the boat entered the harbor, he was gripped by a sense of 'inexpressible well-being,' especially when he heard the sound of the sailors' cries echoing back from the granite cliff-walls as the ship dropped anchor:

> *The sharp rhythm of this call stayed with me as a powerful, comforting omen, and it soon shaped itself into the sailors' theme in my 'Fliegende Holländer', the idea for which I was already carrying in my head.*

Modern musicologists are inclined to treat 'inspiration' stories like this with caution, especially when the source is such an accomplished self-inventor as Wagner. But the weird and atmospheric effect in the opera – where the sailors' cries are answered by echoing horns – is so striking and original that it is hard to dismiss the idea that it was taken from nature itself. True, Wagner originally set the story of *Der Fliegende Holländer* in Scotland, and only changed it to Norway (with a specific reference to Sandviken) weeks before the premiere. Nevertheless, he may have had any number of reasons for choosing Scotland initially (the country, after all, has more potent literary associations for the German Romantics than does Norway); in any case this is hardly devastating evidence against the *Mein Leben* story. Wagner may have romanticized the genesis of the sailors' theme a little, but romanticizing and pure invention are not synonymous.

An Auspicious Meeting?

The *Thetis* finally docked in London, where Wagner tried without success to introduce himself to the Philharmonic Society's conductor Sir George Smart and to Edward Bulwer-Lytton, whose novel had formed the basis of Wagner's *Rienzi*. Disappointed, Wagner sailed with Minna across the English Channel to the French port of Boulogne, where at once Wagner's luck seemed to change. Meyerbeer himself was visiting Boulogne and received Wagner with great kindness. He showed a gratifying interest in the younger composer's work, promising to recommend him to the director of the Paris Opéra and to its much-admired conductor, François Habeneck. Meyerbeer's interest appears to have been sincere enough, which makes Wagner's later hostility towards him even harder to stomach.

It must have seemed to Wagner that he had 'pitched' **Rienzi** correctly with a view to performance on the Parisian stage. Here, what we now call 'Grand Opera' reigned supreme, with Meyerbeer's own operas very much to the fore. Wagner soon came to see Parisian Grand Opera, with its formulaic reliance on historical or mythic plots, clearly separated arias, duets and trios, its ostentatious choruses and sumptuous ballets, and its almost invariable division into five-act structures, as intolerably limited and restrictive. At this stage, however, he was determined not only to master the idiom, but to take it to new heights, as he later recalled:

> *'Grand opera', with all its scenic and musical splendor, its effect-ridden, musically massive strength of passion, stood before me; my artistic ambition demanded not merely that I should imitate it, but that I should outdo all previous examples with sumptuous extravagance.*

33

In all of this, *Rienzi* is, on the whole, true Grand Opera. That said, one begins to sense something of Wagner's impatience with the stylistic limitations he had imposed on himself. Recitatives become more expressive, more dramatic, and less easy to distinguish from the arias and other 'numbers' that follow them. The orchestra too is becoming less of an accompanist (however splendid) to the singing, and more of a commentator on the feelings and actions of the leading characters. However, we are still a long way from the psychological insight of *Tristan* and the *Ring*, or even from parts of *Die Fliegende Holländer*.

But Paris turned out to be a bitter disappointment. Although there were valuable experiences (not least a revelatory performance of the first three movements of Beethoven's Ninth Symphony under Habeneck), Wagner's two-and-a-half years in the French capital are a painful story of professional failure, the experience of which heightened his tendencies to depression, resentment, and paranoia. The revolution of 1830 had soon shown itself to be a false dawn: the Paris of King Louis-Philippe was a society where elites and cliques ruled and money talked; the cultural climate favored glittering, superficial entertainment, not 'natural' expression and radical politics.

Paris turned out to be a bitter disappointment.

At first Wagner's luck appeared to be holding. In 1840 the Théâtre de la Renaissance took on *Das Liebesverbot*; but, almost immediately, the theatre went bankrupt. In later years Wagner was to see Meyerbeer's handiwork even in this piece of pure bad luck. But initially his attempts to court the older composer's favors were embarrassing in their sycophancy and self-abasement. He routinely called Meyerbeer 'master', signing himself 'your slave', and even 'your property'. This developed into an almost manic flattery:

It is Meyerbeer *and* Meyerbeer *alone, and you will readily understand me when I tell you that I weep tears of the deepest emotion whenever I think of the man who is everything to me, everything.*

In May 1840, when he wrote the above-quoted letter, Wagner's fortunes had plummeted to such an extreme that he may have been on the verge of losing his mental balance. It is hard to know what the shrewd, worldly Meyerbeer made of expressions such as these; he nevertheless continued to try to help Wagner – and although he was unsuccessful in this, there is little evidence to support Wagner's later accusations towards Meyerbeer of hypocrisy and deviousness. So how did Wagner's suspicion of him take root? It is likely that Meyerbeer's polished demeanor, summed up in the poet W.B. Yeats's image of the 'smiling public man', made Wagner's hackles rise. Meyerbeer has been described by several writers as a master of PR long before the term was invented. Such people inevitably provoke resentment and suspicion. But in one of Wagner's sudden, surprising shafts of insight, he seems to have realized that the humiliations he suffered in Paris had colored his judgement. Meyerbeer, he wrote, had been 'perpetually kind', but he reminded Wagner of 'the darkest – I might almost say the most wicked – period of my life, when he [Meyerbeer] still made a show of protecting me; it was a period of connections and back-staircases'.

It was also a period of hack-work, poverty, and almost continual disappointment. Although the newly completed *Rienzi* was submitted to the Paris Opéra at the end of 1840, the management was non-committal. Efforts to interest the Opéra in *Rienzi*'s successor, *Der Fliegende Holländer*, resulted in a double humiliation: performance was ruled out, but the new

> Wagner's fortunes had plummeted to such an extreme that he may have been on the verge of losing his mental balance.

Wagner in Paris as a young man. Drawing by E.B. Kietz, signed 1842

director, Léon Pillet, persuaded the desperately hard-up Wagner to sell his libretto so that another composer might set it to music. Wagner did manage to make a small, intermittent income by arranging other composers' work and writing articles, but his and Minna's quality of life grew worse and worse.In winter the cold forced them to live entirely in one room, Wagner retreating to bed whenever he was not at his desk. At one point the noise of nearby metalworkers nearly drove him to distraction. He may even have spent a short time in prison for debt. All this Wagner suffered while the peddlers of what he was coming to see as vacuous, superficial musical entertainment seemed to grow richer and richer. Noting how several of these were, like Meyerbeer, Jewish, he fell back on the dubious comfort of the racial conspiracy theory – rather that than admit that the world's musical capital simply didn't want him.

New Friends, New Ideas

If Paris was a professional disaster for Wagner, there were rewards on a more private scale. Wagner struck up what was to be an immensely important friendship with the renowned Hungarian pianist–composer Franz Liszt. He also met the great German poet Heinrich Heine, one of whose writings had given Wagner the idea for the story of the doomed Dutch mariner in *Der Fliegende Holländer*. That Heine was also Jewish does not seem to have bothered Wagner at all. Neither did the Jewishness of a new close friend, the philologist Samuel Lehrs, of whom Wagner always spoke with great warmth and gratitude. Lehrs introduced Wagner to some of the most important radical writings of the day, including the anarchist philosopher Pierre-Joseph Proudhon's

If Paris was a professional disaster for Wagner, there were rewards on a more private scale. Wagner struck up what was to be an immensely important friendship with the renowned Hungarian pianist–composer Franz Liszt.

Qu'est-ce que la propriété? ('What Is Property?'), from which comes the famous line 'Property is theft'.

It was also probably Lehrs who drew Wagner's attention to Ludwig Feuerbach's *Das Wesen des Christentums* ('The Essence of Christianity'). Feuerbach had raised debate about the validity of religion into a new sphere. While God or the gods may have no objective reality, religion may be 'true' in another sense. Human beings make gods in their own image: they are projections of fundamental human characteristics onto a cosmic screen. As such they have great value: they can tell us important things about our own nature – things it might not be easy, or even possible, to express in other terms. For Feuerbach, as it now was for Wagner too, the central importance of love in the world's great religions was crucial. Through religion, mankind has revealed what it is that carries the greatest significance for us. At the core of religious myth, said Feuerbach, can the true morality be found.

Hearing Beethoven's Ninth Symphony performed well, even without the all-important choral finale, was another formative experience. Wagner worked out some of his thoughts and feelings about it in an essay entitled *Eine Pilgerfahrt zu Beethoven* ('A Pilgrimage to Beethoven', 1840). In this he put his own developing ideas into the mouth of the great German composer. Purely instrumental music had reached the limits of possibility with the first three movements of the Ninth Symphony; after this the only way forward was for music to be 'fertilized' by poetry. Beethoven had striven towards a new relationship between words, music, and drama in his opera *Fidelio*: however fine the music (and *Fidelio* contains some of the finest music in the operatic repertoire), the story, the character development and, above all, the ideals expressed were every bit as important. Yet Wagner felt that Beethoven had only partly succeeded.

Hearing Beethoven's Ninth Symphony performed well, even without the all-important choral finale, was another formative experience.

The Beethoven portrayed by Wagner in *Eine Pilgerfahrt* is fully aware of this, and of the reason why:

> *Were I to make opera after my own heart, then people would run away from it, for it would have no arias, duets, trios, or any of the other stuff with which operas are patched together today. What I would want to put in its place no singer would sing and no audience would hear, for they know nothing but glittering lies, brilliant nonsense and sugared boredom.*

The voice of Wagner and the imprint of his recent Parisian experience are only too audible in that last sentence. In *Eine Pilgerfahrt* 'Beethoven' now outlines his theory for the ideal coming-together of music and words:

> *Musical instruments represent the primal voices of creation and nature. What they express can never be clearly defined, for they embody the primal feelings themselves as they emerge from the chaos of the first creation... It is quite different with the genius of the human voice: this represents man's heart and its definite individual emotions. Its character is therefore limited, but defined and clear. So now bring these two elements together – unite them! Set against the wild, inchoate, undefined primal feeling, as represented by the instruments, the clear definite emotion of the human heart, as represented by the voice. The introduction of this second element will smooth out and calm the conflicts of the primal feelings, will turn their flood into a defined, integrated course; while the human heart, taking into itself those primal feelings, will be infinitely strengthened and enlarged, able to feel clearly its earlier vague intuition of the Highest transformed into godlike consciousness.*

The resolution of a great 'flood' of primal feeling into defined human utterance, which Wagner saw in the grand overall scheme of Beethoven's Ninth, was to find equally original expression in the Prelude and first scene of *Das Rheingold*, just over a decade later.

Possibly just as important for Wagner was his hearing of the French composer Hector Berlioz's 'dramatic symphony' *Roméo et Juliette*. This astonishing hybrid work – a gigantic fusion of symphony, tone poem, and dramatic cantata, with a finale more like the concluding scene of a grand Romantic opera – also left a deep imprint on Wagner. Indeed the famous yearning motif that opens and subsequently pervades Wagner's *Tristan und Isolde* bears more than a passing resemblance to a sighing figure from the 'Romeo Alone' section of Berlioz's symphony (though what Wagner draws from it is still more original). Berlioz's Romantic high seriousness was deeply unfashionable in Paris in the early 1840s, which probably drew Wagner all the more deeply towards him. In later years Wagner was often dismissive of *Roméo et Juliette* ('Piles of rubbish heaped on the most beautiful inventions' was a characteristic remark); but then Wagner was always inclined to belittle those from whose music he had learned, Meyerbeer very much included. One wonders if he would have been quite so liberal in his praise of Beethoven in 1840 if that great inspirational figure had still been alive.

Whatever the case, Wagner soon began work on a dramatic symphony of his own, based on the story of Faust, the scholar who sells his soul to the devil: a story immortalized by Goethe but with its roots deep in German folk history. The symphony was never completed, but the first movement from 1840 survives, in a revision of fifteen years later, as Wagner's **Eine Faust-Ouvertüre** ('A Faust Overture'). It is a powerful orchestral fantasy which more than hints at

CD 2
track 4

www.naxosbooks.com

great things to come.

'Through Adversity to the Stars'

By the spring of 1841 Wagner had finally finished work on the libretto for **Der Fliegende Holländer**. Some musical numbers were already written; even so, Wagner's completion of the score between May and July is impressive, especially given his struggles to support himself and Minna. Poverty does not appear to have stopped Wagner's musical thoughts from pouring out onto paper. At the end of the **Overture to Der Fliegende Holländer**, which he composed last, he wrote 'Per aspera at astra. Gott geb's' – 'Through adversity to the stars. God willing.'

Der Fliegende Holländer marks a huge step forward in Wagner's development as a music dramatist. It still lags some way behind the ideal as spelt out in *Eine Pilgerfahrt zu Beethoven*, as relics remain of the old separate 'numbers' (arias, duets, choruses, ballets, for example), but they are more successfully woven into a continuous thread than in *Rienzi* – creating a kind of drama which at times comes close to being both operatic and symphonic. It is unsurprising that attempts to interest the Parisian opera houses in this groundbreaking work had borne no fruit. But by the time Wagner finished *Der Fliegende Holländer*, uplifting news arrived from another quarter: *Rienzi* had been accepted for performance, not in Paris but at the Royal Saxon Court Theatre in Wagner's old home town of Dresden. Ironically, Meyerbeer had been influential in bringing this about, but he was to receive no thanks for his efforts.

Thoroughly disillusioned with Paris, Wagner decided to head back to Germany. Surprisingly, he and Minna were still together. The strains on their relationship, including her earlier infidelity, had been appalling, and there were reports of

Website

www.naxosbooks.com

CD 1
track 1

www.naxosbooks.com

terrible scenes. Fundamentally, however, Minna had remained loyal to Wagner, even though she must have found his failures in Paris and their mounting debts just as galling as he did. And she had not yet been put to the ultimate test by Wagner's own adulterous passions. She set off with him to Dresden in April 1842, still apparently believing in his talents and earning potential.

Return to the Fatherland

The interest shown in *Rienzi* in Dresden no doubt confirmed all Wagner's feelings against France and in favor of his homeland. Among his own people he would surely be appreciated. Crossing the River Rhine – always a potent national symbol for Germans – produced a powerful release of emotion: 'I saw the Rhine for the first time; with tears swelling in my eyes I, a poor artist, swore eternal loyalty to my German fatherland.' Not long after he had crossed the Rhine he was granted a splendid view of Wartburg Castle overlooking the town of Eisenach in Thuringia. He had already encountered the story of the medieval singing competition at the Wartburg, in which a nobleman contests in song for the hand of the ruler's daughter. Seeing the castle, perched high amid mountains, was another impression that lasted: it was to become the setting for Acts II and III of *Tannhäuser*.

The good omens continued. Soon after arriving in Dresden, Wagner made his way to Berlin where there was firm discussion about a performance of *Der Fliegende Holländer* – again on Meyerbeer's recommendation. The plans fell through when the old Intendant, Count Redern, retired and was replaced by the much less enthusiastic Theodor von

The interest shown in *Rienzi* in Dresden no doubt confirmed all Wagner's feelings against France and in favor of his homeland. Among his own people he would surely be appreciated.

Küstner; but even to get this far was more encouraging than anything Wagner had experienced in Paris. In June he, Minna, and her mother had a holiday at the spa town of Teplitz (Teplice) in Bohemia. It was at Teplitz that Wagner's idol Beethoven had famously met Goethe, and had scandalized the great writer and thinker on one of their walks together by refusing to remove his hat and stand aside when the Austrian Empress and entourage went past. If Wagner knew the story, he would have richly appreciated the great man's display of indifference to worldly rank.

It was also at Teplitz that Wagner's ideas for **Tannhäuser** began to take shape. He had already come across a collection of German legends in which the story of the singing contest at Wartburg was ingeniously fused with a separate story – the medieval legend of Tannhäuser, the knight in thrall to Venus who makes a pilgrimage to Rome and is denounced by the Pope. Tannhäuser's rejection of Venus, and the pure amorous pleasure that Venus represents, shows how much Wagner's ideas had changed – or become more complicated – since the celebration of free love in *Das Liebesverbot*. Salvation is now to be found not in erotic abandonment but in the self-sacrificing love of a pure young woman. And yet the music with which Wagner portrays the world of Venus is some of the most brilliantly innovatory – and sensually captivating – that he had yet created. From this time on Wagner's attitude to sexual love was to be strangely paradoxical. He describes its delights (revels in them, even) in some of the most voluptuously beautiful music ever composed: this is even truer of the later, revised version of *Tannhäuser*, in which Venus's music is significantly enriched. Yet alongside this goes a streak of prudishness, a desire for renunciation of worldly pleasure – a longing for something, as Wagner put it, *pure, chaste, virginal and inaccessibly and unfathomably loving... And what else could this loving desire be, this noblest of sentiments that it was in my nature to feel, but the longing to vanish from the present, to perish in that element of infinite love which was unknown on earth, in a way that only death seemed able to achieve.*

Originally Wagner had thought of calling the new opera *Der Venusberg*, but when somebody pointed out that the title – in English 'The Mount of Venus' – might be open to misinterpretation, he was horrified and changed it at once. It was only years later, after he had soaked himself in the philosophy of Schopenhauer, that Wagner was able to work through that paradox creatively. It would find definitive expression in what many see as his supreme masterpiece, *Tristan und Isolde*. In 1842, however, that musical mastery and psychological insight were still some way off.

On his return to Dresden from Teplitz, there were the rehearsals for *Rienzi* to be attended to; the performance was booked for October 20. The first signs were promising, and Wagner was soon on close terms with the stage manager and chorus master Wilhelm Fischer and the costume designer Ferdinand Heine. Interest was growing outside the theatre too, partly because the still celebrated soprano Wilhelmine Schröder-Devrient had agreed to take the (male) part of Adriano – a so-called 'trouser-role'. Perhaps also the participants had begun to sense that there was something about *Rienzi* that reflected a mood spreading among the German states at that time. While the post-revolutionary Parisian bourgeoisie frittered its time away on distracting, luxurious entertainment, the liberal German middle classes were abuzz with talk of democracy, a free press, and national unity. Could it be that the story of the idealistic Roman tribune

Chapter 3

Triumph and Disaster

Triumph and Disaster

CD 1
track 6

www.naxosbooks.com

A scene from
the premiere of
Rienzi *at Dresden*
Hoftheater on
October 20, 1842

Rienzi was indeed a huge success – the first in Wagner's composing career, and also the last unqualified success he was to experience for many years. That *Rienzi* should have been the most successful of his operas before the complete *Ring* cycle appeared in 1876 will surprise some readers, as it is far from being a favorite today. Charles Rosen, author of *The Romantic Generation*, has called it 'Meyerbeer's worst opera', and it is arguable that *Rienzi* owes a lot to the composer whom Wagner had begun to turn against.

Rienzi's immense length (nearly five hours of music) is one factor that has weighed against it in recent times. In Wagner's day it quickly became the practice to perform it in two halves, on two separate nights; but even in that form it has failed to endear itself to modern audiences. Part of the problem appears to be that the musical interest, despite some effective moments, is stretched a good deal more thinly than in Wagner's first two operas. He relies too much on what he later called 'massive' effects and 'sumptuous extravagance'. For a few writers, this problem of the general tone of *Rienzi* has more sinister implications. Theodor Adorno noted its 'self-praise and pomp', which for him were unquestionably 'emblems of fascism'. Wagner's authoritative biographer Barry Millington complains of 'a tendency to cudgel listeners, to overwhelm them with accumulating banks of sound', which is 'intensified in *Rienzi* to an unparalleled degree'. Others point to the fact that *Rienzi* was an important early influence on Hitler –which may for some be enough to confirm Adorno's charge of operatic fascism.

Perhaps the issue is more complicated than that. One of the most insightful comments on Wagner's tendency to 'overwhelm', to intimidate some listeners, is found in Bryan Magee's *Wagner and Philosophy*:

> *[Wagner's] music has an enormously powerful drive of assertiveness that seems to be sweeping everything before it, an unremitting vehemence that never for one moment lets up. More than any other characteristic of Wagner's music it is the one that those who dislike it react against most and repudiate... they say they feel as if Wagner is trying to impose himself on them forcibly, to subordinate their wills, to subjugate them. When people claim that there is something fascist about his music, this is what they are usually referring*

> *Rienzi's* immense length (nearly five hours) has weighed against it in recent times.

47

to.

For other listeners, says Magee, the experience of listening to Wagner's music has a completely different effect:

> *Others who love [the music] feel unthreatened by it [this quality], yet they know it to be there – however, far from feeling subjugated they feel liberated, perhaps because the music expresses something they would like to be able to express themselves but cannot: it is speaking out of what is inside them, and thus is speaking for them.*

The twentieth-century German philosopher Ernst Bloch said, 'When we listen to music, what we are really hearing is ourselves.' For the young Adolf Hitler, *Rienzi* clearly spoke out of what was inside him: will to power and overweening political ambition. For the liberal-leaning middle-class Germans who attended *Rienzi*'s premiere in October 1842 the story of the great but tragic Roman reformer appears to have spoken out of their growing desire for democracy, freedom and justice. *Rienzi* may be a difficult work to love, but it does contain some fine music, especially the noble theme of Rienzi's prayer in Act V, which features prominently in the Overture. A melody like that would surely stir the Dresden audience to sympathy with the opera's heroic but tragically flawed hero.

CD 1
track 1

www.naxosbooks.com

Website

www.naxosbooks.com

A 'Storm-Swept Ballad'

In the wake of *Rienzi*'s towering success, it was a relatively simple matter for Wagner to arrange a Dresden premiere for **Der fliegende Holländer**, and this followed on January 2, 1843. The reception was far from cold, but Wagner sensed, probably correctly, that the public who had thrilled to *Rienzi* were somewhat disappointed by its brooding 'storm-swept' successor. If *Rienzi*'s content is unmistakably political, that of *Der Fliegende Holländer* is psychological. In place of the great reformer is a doomed, tormented outsider; the action of *Holländer*, instead of being carried forward by a tide of popular feeling, is propelled by something much more raw and elemental: the sea. That Wagner was able to portray the ocean with a strength and imaginative audacity unparalleled in any musical nature-portrait before him (with the possible exception of the 'Storm' movement in Beethoven's 'Pastoral' Symphony) doesn't seem to have been enough to sway the Dresden audience. When the work was heard again, at the Berlin Royal Opera in January 1844, it met with hostility. Wagner was deeply wounded by some of the comments he read in the press, and it helped to form his lasting hatred of critics.

Der Fliegende Holländer is nevertheless a much better work than *Rienzi*: far more concise, stylistically more sophisticated, deeper in its characterization and nowhere near as indebted to the grand operatic examples of Meyerbeer and his contemporary Gaspare Spontini (another name rarely seen on theatre billings today, but in his time enormously influential).

Before this humiliation in Berlin, the thirty-year-old Wagner had decided that the time was right to publish an *Autobiographische Skizze* ('Autobiographical Sketch'). His desire to introduce himself in this way to the German people, who had heard nothing of him during his years in Königsberg, Riga and Paris, might be seen as a timely piece of self-promotion. With the triumph of *Rienzi* still a recent memory, Wagner was prevailed upon by Weber's widow to accept the position of Kapellmeister at the Court of the King of Saxony. This meant that Wagner would be

> *Der Fliegende Holländer* is a much better work than *Rienzi*: more concise and more sophisticated.

responsible for not only the music of the royal chapel but also court opera and orchestral performances. The post was shared, but the other Kapellmeister, Karl Gottlieb Reissiger, was no obstacle to Wagner's acceptance – for it was Reissiger who had conducted that hugely successful premiere of *Rienzi*. Wagner's initial hesitation in accepting the job seems to have stemmed from his feeling that big changes were needed in the court's musical organization, and that his position would not give him the authority he needed to bring them about. Although the salary offered – 1,500 talers – was acceptable, it was not long before most of it had been eaten up in repaying some of Wagner's more pressing debts.

He was, however, able to use his position to bring more of his own music to the public's attention. In 1843,

Wagner was being courted, somewhat guardedly, by music publishers.

for a coming-together of Saxony's male-voice choral societies, he wrote an ambitious cantata entitled *Das Liebesmahl der Apostel* ('The Love-Feast of the Apostles'), based on the biblical story of the coming of the Holy Ghost at Pentecost. Unfortunately, having the amateur choirs sing mostly unaccompanied, theatrically divided among various parts of Dresden's Frauenkirche, was too much for the abilities of the singers, and Wagner pronounced the effect 'feeble'. It was also at this time that he started work on the music of *Tannhäuser*. In the opera he was able to rework material that he had roughed out in one of his 'occasional' pieces. Its title, *Gruss seiner Treuen an Friedrich August den Geliebten* ('Salute to beloved Friedrich August from his Faithful Subjects'), gives some idea of the kind of attitude Wagner was expected to demonstrate towards his royal employer.

Wagner was now being courted, somewhat guardedly, by music publishers. The respected German firm of Breitkopf & Härtel showed interest in *Rienzi* and *Der Fliegende Holländer*, though when it became clear that they were not offering a fee Wagner decided to publish them himself. Eventually he engaged the Dresden court publisher Meser, a decision he came to regret. Meser had minimal flair when it came to promotion, and his hesitancy cost him valuable sales opportunities, even as Wagner's fame continued to rise. 'If you distilled the quintessence of the most shit-scared, the most unreliable and the most cowardly philistine, what emerges is precisely Meser,' was Wagner's summing-up. More rewarding was throwing himself into a campaign to have Weber's remains brought back from London, where he had died in 1826, to Dresden, where he had been Court Kapellmeister. In supporting the campaign Wagner felt he was repaying a personal debt to Weber: 'He was my true begetter,' Wagner insisted, 'arousing in me a passion for music.' The coffin arrived on December 14, to a torchlit procession with music specially written by Wagner. The composer himself then addressed the crowds with a stirring tribute to Weber as a German national treasure. Once again he appears to have caught the mood admirably.

Holy German Art

Though Wagner did not yet realize it, the honeymoon period with his homeland was coming to an end. The score of *Tannhäuser* was finished in April 1845, after which he set off with Minna for the Bohemian spa town of Marienbad (now Mariánské Lázně in the Czech Republic). His skin complaints had been troubling him again, and he hoped that the healing waters might effect a cure. At the same time he was soaking himself in traditional Germanic legends, looking for more operatic material. The mystically flavored tales of the knights Parzifal and Lohengrin he found especially absorbing.

Wagner was soaking himself in traditional Germanic legends, looking for more operatic material.

CD 2
track 1

www.naxosbooks.com

Website

www.naxosbooks.com

It is also significant that he made his first sketches for the text of **Die Meistersinger von Nürnberg** at around this time, for in a different kind of way this opera, too, is much preoccupied with German national issues. In its final form the opera – the music of which would not be completed for another twenty years – ends with a rousing chorus: 'Ehrt Eure deutschen Meister' ('Honor your German masters'). Again, given the political complexion that nationalism, and especially German nationalism, has acquired in our time it should be noted that the 'masters' Wagner refers to in the final version are artistic, not militaristic. It is Germany's cultural inheritance, and the hope it offers for the future, that Wagner stresses here. The cobbler Hans Sachs's final words to the people of Nuremberg are particularly significant:

> *zerging' in Dunst*
> *das Heil'ge röm'sch Reich,*
> *und bliebe gleich*
> *die heil'ge deutsche Kunst!*

> *Even if the Holy Roman Empire*
> *dissolved in mist,*
> *for us there would still remain*
> *holy German Art!*

CD 1 track 2
CD 2 track 2–3

www.naxosbooks.com

Website

www.naxosbooks.com

The opera's young hero, Walther von Stolzing, is a singer, not a soldier. In any case he is finally upstaged by the figure of Sachs, whose humor, practical wisdom and noble renunciation of his love for the beautiful Eva (whom he freely hands over to Walther) are the most memorable and moving elements in this multi-layered drama.

Also in 1845 Wagner began to draft his opera **Lohengrin**. National concerns are reflected in the opera's political backdrop:

the medieval King of Saxony, Heinrich I, is rallying support among the other German states for a campaign to fend off the threat of invasion from the east. However this recedes into the background as the central issue emerges: the ultimately tragic relationship between Elsa, daughter of the deceased Duke of Brabant, and Lohengrin, the knight of mysterious origins who rescues her when she is unjustly accused of murder. Lohengrin marries Elsa, on condition that she never asks him about his real name and his origins; but in the end the temptation proves too much for her. Reluctantly Lohengrin leaves, and Elsa dies of a broken heart. The people of Brabant meanwhile mourn the loss of the hero who might have led them to victory in battle. The miraculous return of Elsa's brother Gottfried, in gleaming silver raiment, offers some compensation, though Wagner's music hardly embraces this glimmer of hope.

It could be that Wagner was beginning to have doubts about the German people – or at least about their capacity to understand his aims and ideals. Perhaps they were not yet ready for Wagner's version of 'holy German Art'. The first performance of **Tannhäuser** in Dresden in October 1845 turned out to be an even bigger disappointment than *Der Fliegende Holländer*'s premiere. Fourteen years later, Wagner wrote that it was in *Tannhäuser* that he 'first worked with a growing sense of the beautiful, convincing necessity of transition'. Transitions – in which one section flows seamlessly into the next – were to be more frequent and more audacious in the 'Paris' revision of *Tannhäuser*, but they are here in the opera's original form, along with Wagner's increasingly ambiguous, chromatic harmonic thinking and sophisticated use of the orchestra in the Overture and in Venus's music. All of this was, it seems, too much for the Dresdeners.

Wagner's increasingly sophisticated use of the orchestra was, it seems, too much for the Dresdeners.

Meanwhile Wagner's efforts to bring about change in the musical organization at the royal court were meeting entrenched opposition. His report *Die Königliche Kapelle betreffend* ('Concerning the Royal Orchestra'), submitted to the court authorities in March 1846, was full of practical, and indeed humane, suggestions as to how the administration of the orchestra could be improved and the working life of the musicians made more bearable – but tact and diplomacy were never Wagner's strong points. The report met with no success, and this must have hit hard. Energetically self-assertive though Wagner was, there was always the contrary tendency to depression, and his confidence was always brittle. He had a constant need for reassurance behind the seemingly arrogant self-promotion. For years afterwards he would agonize about *Tannhäuser*: he revised it again and again, and was even talking about returning to it not long before he died. And when two friends expressed doubts about the ending of Wagner's next opera *Lohengrin*, he was seriously disturbed and only regained his assurance about the work after receiving sensitively expressed encouragement from the wife of the Intendant at the Dresden court. As was so often the case, womanly reassurance carried weight with Wagner in time of need.

For years he would agonize about *Tannhäuser*: he revised it again and again.

The Greek Ideal

There were artistic triumphs from these years, though these mostly centered on Wagner's conducting rather than his own compositions. In 1846 a performance on Palm Sunday of Beethoven's Ninth Symphony, including the choral finale, was a tremendous success; Wagner's demand for extra rehearsal time was seen to have been utterly justified. Also successful was a performance in January 1847 of Gluck's opera *Iphigénie en Aulide*, given in Wagner's new version which had extra music linking some of the separate arias and choruses. Wagner was impressed by the great eighteenth-century German composer's attempts to make opera less sectional and create a more continuous dramatic flow – in this regard he would have seen Gluck as his own forerunner.

All this time he was continuing to work on *Lohengrin*, and busying himself with a study of the Ancient Greek playwrights. Aeschylus' great trilogy *The Oresteia* made a particularly powerful impression. Wagner would draw encouragement from Aeschylus' depiction of the story of the hero Orestes in three full-length plays when he gave the *Ring* its final form as a trilogy – or 'tetralogy', with *Das Rheingold* as a 'preliminary evening' ('Vorabend').

> The Greece of Aeschylus' day, he felt, was the only time in history when art had lived up to its full potential.

More importantly, Wagner was moving away from the Romantics' idealization of the Greeks towards a bolder con-ception of his own. The Greece of Aeschylus' day, he felt, was the only time in history when art had lived up to its full potential. Not only did works like *The Oresteia* present universal truths about human beings as individuals through the use of myth, they gave expression to their collective needs as members of a nation. Furthermore, they brought together several art forms – singing, dance, instrumental music, poetry, mime – in a grand synthesis. As Wagner put it in 1849, in an essay entitled *Die Kunst und die Revolution* ('Art and Revolution'):

> *With the Greeks the perfect work of art, the drama, was the sum and substance of all that could be expressed in the Greek nature; it was – in intimate connection with its history – the nation itself that stood facing itself in the work of art,*

becoming conscious of itself, and, in the space of a few hours,
rapturously devouring, as it were, its own essence.

Wagner now saw it as his mission to recreate 'the perfect work of art' for his time. Since then, argued Wagner, the separation of the arts – their splitting-off into seemingly self-sufficient entities – had been a process of sorry decline. By becoming separated, the art forms had also been emasculated, emptied of their true spiritual content, and, worst of all, had ultimately fallen victim to commercialism. Wagner now saw it as his mission to reunite them, to recreate 'the perfect work of art' for his time. It would take more thinking, more reading, and more working over his ideas in literary form before he felt able to undertake this extraordinarily ambitious program, but the way ahead became clearer during those Dresden years.

The Revolutionary

At the beginning of 1848, Wagner's mother died. Visiting her on her deathbed Wagner was deeply moved, and he also began to realize that with her death his connections with his family were over. Minna, though still apparently faithful, did not offer the support and understanding he craved. He was now on his own, artistically and personally. Work offered consolation. *Lohengrin* was progressing well, and Wagner gave successful performances of Bach's motet *Singet dem Herrn* ('Sing to the Lord') and the *Stabat Mater* by the Renaissance master Palestrina. In putting on works from what was then seen as the remote past, musically speaking, Wagner was ahead of his time. Though others, like Mendelssohn, had begun to revive interest in Bach's music, it was still seen as very much a connoisseur's taste, while Renaissance choral music was barely heard at all. Both these works left a lasting impression on Wagner, however:

witness the very Bachian treatment of a Lutheran hymn tune in the opening scene of *Die Meistersinger*, or the freely floating choral polyphony, with its highly theatrical placing of the voices on- and off-stage, in *Parsifal* – such 'antiphonal' effects are foreshadowed by Palestrina in the *Stabat Mater*.

Wagner was also putting energy into more political projects. In May 1848 he handed over his *Entwurf zur Organisation eines deutschen Nationaltheaters* ('Plan for the Organization of a German National Theatre') to the court authorities. This was to be a democratically run institution, with resident writers and composers as well as musicians, and an associated drama and music school, all under the direction of one Kapellmeister – for which role Wagner recommended himself. The royal dignitaries were profoundly unimpressed. Still more provocative was his overtly political tract *Wie verhalten sich republikanische Bestrebungen dem Königthume gegenüber?* ('How Do Republican Endeavors Stand in Relation to the Monarchy?'). The mere mention of republicanism was a red rag to the royal bull; but although Wagner condemned out-and-out revolution (the monarchy still had a role to play in the composer's utopia), his predictions of the downfall of the aristocracy brought instant demands for his dismissal.

> Wagner took elements of his *Ring* story from Icelandic epics that tell of the Viking gods and their downfall.

At the same time he was hard at work on a plan to turn the ancient legend of the Ring of the Nibelungs into a Greek-inspired music drama. He found material for his reworked legend in a variety of sources, not all of them specifically German. The account of the last days of the hero Siegfried came largely from the medieval German epic poem *Das Nibelungenlied*, but Wagner also took elements of his *Ring* story from the somewhat earlier Icelandic epics known as the 'Poetic Edda' and the 'Prose Edda', which tell of the Viking gods and their downfall, and from the Icelandic *Völsunga saga*, in which a Siegfried-like hero is portrayed as 'Sigurd'. From these emerged Wagner's first sketches for a libretto on the story of the Germanic hero Siegfried, the hero who took on the chief of the gods himself and brought about the end of his corrupt regime – a fitting subject for a nationalistic revolutionary opera.

There were also sketches for another possible opera, *Jesus von Nazareth*, in which the revolutionary aspects of Christ's teachings and life would be stressed: in particular, his denunciation of money as the root of all evil and his acting-out to the last of the principle of self-sacrificing love.

Wagner's ideas seem all the more provocative, indeed dangerous, when seen against the political background of the years 1848–9. Once again, unrest was brewing up all over the continent of Europe. In France there was another revolution, this time empowered not so much by the liberal bourgeoisie as by the working classes – a phenomenon duly noted by the young Karl Marx. King Louis-Philippe was forced to abdicate, and there was an attempt to set up a republic based on the principles of the leading socialist thinker Louis Blanc. Louis Napoleon, nephew of the original revolutionary hero, was elected president by a huge majority. In a short time this too was to prove another false dawn, but for the moment revolutionary sympathizers like Wagner were jubilant. Closer to home there was more exciting news. In Austria Prince Klemens von Metternich, one of the leading figures in the Congress of Vienna and vigorous opponent of liberalism, was forced to resign from the Foreign Ministry, and attempts were made to set up a new democratic parliament in Frankfurt. Before very long the Frankfurt Parliament was beginning to think more in terms of *Realpolitik* than of revolution. In March 1849 the new 'national'

In France, Louis Napoleon, nephew of the original revolutionary hero, was elected president. Revolutionary sympathizers like Wagner were jubilant.

assembly offered the crown of a notional new Germany to the King of Prussia, Friedrich Wilhelm IV, the thinking being that Protestant Prussia represented a better hope for the future than reactionary, Roman Catholic Austria. Friedrich Wilhelm was contemptuously dismissive. He had other plans: soon afterwards Prussian troops disbanded the Parliament and reimposed order on conservative lines, to Prussia's advantage.

> Wagner's revolutionary thinking appears to have intensified during this extraordinary period.

By this time many radicals had begun to lose hope, but not Wagners. Indeed his revolutionary thinking appears to have intensified during this extraordinary period. No doubt this was partly the consequence of an important new friendship. At some point in 1848–9 Wagner was intro-duced by his friend and former fellow-Kapellmeister August Röckel to the most notorious anarchist revolutionary of the nineteenth century, the Russian Mikhail Bakunin. Physically imposing, Bakunin was every bit as powerful and self-assertive a man as Wagner, but the two seem to have derived a lot of stimulation from each other's company. They shared a love of music, but differed radically as to the role of art in any forthcoming revolution. For Bakunin, art was irrelevant to the struggle in hand. Wagner's recollections of this charismatic, bear-like man make fascinating reading. He describes Bakunin as 'a truly likeable and sensitive person', but the Russian's vision of the destruction to come both excited and appalled him:

> *In this remarkable man the purest humanitarianism was combined with a savagery utterly inimical to all culture, and thus my relationship with him fluctuated between instinctive horror and irresistible attraction... The annihilation of all civilization was the objective on which he had set his heart; to use all political levers as a means to this end was his current*

preoccupation, and it often served him as a pretext for ironic merriment.

The celebration of self-sacrificing love that Wagner planned to portray in *Jesus von Nazareth* only provoked more grim humor in Bakunin: the execution of the 'weak' Jesus was more black comedy than tragedy. And yet the notion of razing everything to the ground in order to begin again did appeal to something very deep in Wagner. This was a man who had already half-concluded – as would Pierre Boulez a century later – that the best way to deal with opera houses, for instance, might be to blow them all up; if that meant that the whole of Paris was destroyed in the process, so much the better. It is of the utmost importance to remember that this was the crucible in which Wagner's ideas for the *Ring* were

Wagner's writings were becoming ever more inflammatory.

forming. Brünnhilde's final act of self-immolation, which brings down Valhalla and ends the rule of the gods, has its origins partly in those alarming but so exciting conversations with Bakunin, all of which happened while Europe appeared to be in the process of turning itself upside down.

Wagner's writings were becoming ever more inflammatory. In March 1848 he published a poem *Die Not* ('Nec-essity') in Röckel's republican journal *Volksblätter* ('The People's Paper'). Then, after the Frankfurt Parliament's failure to enlist the support of Friedrich Wilhelm of Prussia, a still more thunderous broadside appeared, entitled *Die Revolution*. This was printed anonymously, but modern scholars broadly agree that the penmanship was almost certainly Wagner's; the short extract that follows gives some idea of the tone. In it the use of the personal pronoun is telling: the writer sees himself as, in effect, the incarnation of the revolutionary spirit:

I will destroy every evil that has power over mankind. I will

destroy the domination of one over another, of the dead over
the living; I will shatter the power of the mighty, of the law
and of property. Man's sole master shall be his own *will, his*
only law his own *desire, his only property his* own *strength,*
for only the free man is holy and there is nothing higher
than he. *Let there be an end to the evil that gives one man*
power over millions... since all are equal I shall destroy every
dominion of one over another.

It is not clear what active role Wagner played in the Dresden
uprising that followed in 1849. In *Mein Leben* he portrays himself
as a figure on the sidelines, one who was with
the insurrectionists in spirit rather than in
action. But Wagner, who began writing *Mein*
Leben in 1865, would have wished to play down
his part in the conflict – anxious, for one thing,
not to embarrass his newly acquired patron,
King Ludwig II of Bavaria.

> It is not clear what active role
> Wagner played in the Dresden
> uprising in 1849. The King of
> Saxony stated that if Wagner
> had been caught, he would
> probably have been
> sentenced to death

In Dresden, as in Frankfurt, it was
the forces of the state that won the
day. The uprising was brutally suppressed. Bakunin
and Wagner's friend Röckel were arrested. Röckel was
sentenced to death, the sentence later reduced to life
imprison-ment (he in the end served thirteen years of his
sentence). The King of Saxony some years afterwards stated
that if Wagner had been caught, he would probably have been
sentenced to death along with Röckel. Among
the accusations formally brought against Wagner were that
he had spied on royal troops and been involved in the making
of hand grenades. There is a rich historical irony here: while
Wagner was apparently preparing to man the barricades, his
future philosophical hero Arthur Schopenhauer (then living in
Frankfurt) was doing his bit to help the counter-revolutionary
forces in their violent efforts to put down what he called the

The warrant issued for Wagner's arrest in 1849

'rabble' and the 'sovereign *canaille*' – by which he meant the Revolution's intellectual leaders as much as the 'mob' that followed them.

A Wanted Man

Wagner had escaped arrest at first by pure luck: he was late for the coach in which Röckel tried to make his getaway and the troops therefore missed him. But flight was clearly a matter of some urgency. Wagner managed to get to Weimar, where he was generously sheltered by Liszt. Then the arrest warrant was published and Wagner realized that he would have to flee the country – not just Saxony, but any of the lands in what had been the old German Confederation. Liszt recommended Paris, but on arrival there Wagner found the city's musical life just as bad as before: artistically it was as though the Revolution of 1848 had never happened. So Wagner settled on Zurich, which was German-speaking, but independent of Saxon or Prussian influence.

> Wagner realized that he would have to flee the country. Liszt recommended Paris, but on arrival there Wagner found the city's musical life just as bad as before.

He had not yet despaired of the Revolution. Paradoxically he retained hope that the spark of the Paris uprising might be flickering among the wreckage, ready to spring to flame again given the right encouragement. Art could still be the vital regenerative force. He set down his hopes and ideas in another essay, finished on arrival in Zurich in November 1849: *Das Kunstwerk der Zukunft* ('The Artwork of the Future'). It still strikes a ringingly – desperately – optimistic note. As with his toe-curling flattery of Meyerbeer during his Paris years, there is something almost manic about Wagner's determination to look boldly to the notion of an ideal future, to cling to his idea of a Greek-inspired religion of art.

It is our task to make out of Greek art the completely human art; to remove from it the conditions under which it was precisely a Greek, and not a completely human *art; to widen the* garb of religion, *in which alone it was communal Greek art, after the removal of which, as a selfish individual art species, it could not longer fulfil the need of the community, but only that of luxury – however beautiful! – to widen this garb of the specifically* Greek religion *to the bond of the religion of the future – that of* universality *– in order to form for ourselves a true conception of the artwork of the future. Yet, wretched as we are, it is precisely the power to bring about this unity, this* religion of the future, *that we lack. For after all, no matter how many of us feel this urge towards the artwork of the future, we are* singular *and* individual. *An artwork is religion brought to life; religions, however, are created, not by the artist, but by the people.*

Let us then be content that for the present – without egoistic vanity, without wishing to seek satisfaction in any selfish illusion whatsoever, but with sincere and loving resignation to the hope for the artwork of the future – we test first of all the nature of the art varieties which today, in their dismembered, separate condition, make up the present state of art; that we brace ourselves for this test by a glance at the art of the Greeks; and that we then boldly and confidently draw our conditions as to the great universal artwork of the future!'

Wagner was now an exile, a wanted man, under possible sentence of death in his homeland. The revolutionary spirit had been crushed, and the German lands were beginning to move towards a different future from the one his radical mind envisaged.

For all his talk of 'sincere and loving resignation', did Wagner have any idea in November 1849 of the enormity of the task ahead of him? He was now an exile, a wanted man, under possible sentence of death in his homeland. There was not the remotest possibility of going back and exploiting *Rienzi*'s triumph to the advantage

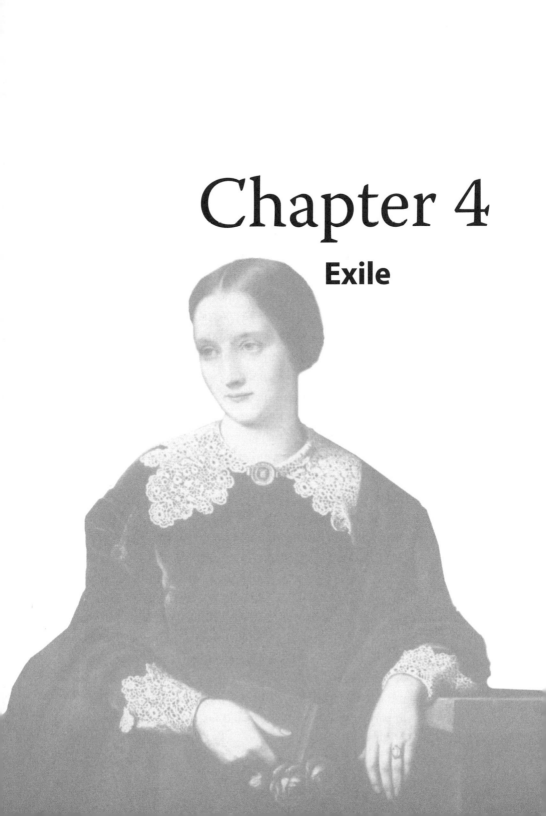

Chapter 4

Exile

Exile

Minna joined Wagner in Zurich – reluctantly – towards the end of 1849. For his revolutionary activities she had nothing but scorn, especially since they had resulted in her husband's throwing away his Royal Kapellmeister status and salary. However, at this stage she still tried to help him salvage his composing career. When Liszt recommended that Wagner make one last attempt to score a hit on the Parisian stage she backed him resolutely. Wagner duly began to make plans for an opera entitled *Wieland der Schmied* ('Wieland the Smith'), about a brilliant metalworker who is taken captive by his enemies but is helped to escape by a faithful, loving woman – unmistakable echoes of Wagner's own fate and hopes.

On returning to Paris he quickly recognized that he would find no market for such an opera, but there came a point during his Parisian trip when his luck seemed about to change in another direction. He met two passionate female admirers: Julie Ritter, a widow he had known in Dresden, and Jessie Laussot, an Englishwoman unhappily married to a French wine merchant. Could redemption be arriving in female form – as it had for Wieland, and for the doomed Dutchman in *Der fliegende Holländer*? Jessie in particular adored Wagner and his music, and showed an

During his Parisian trip his luck seemed about to change. He met two passionate female admirers.

understanding of his ideals that surprised and thrilled him. Inevitably they were soon having a passionate affair. There was talk of elopement to Greece; more solidly, Jessie Laussot and Julie Richter clubbed together to offer Wagner an allowance of 3,000 francs per annum. Then Jessie's husband found out about their relationship and informed the police that a dangerous revolutionary was in their midst. So Wagner had to hurry back to Zurich in July. Julie Ritter was able to offer a rather smaller allowance, which she faithfully continued until 1859, but it was small change for a man with Wagner's tastes and ambitions. Back in Zurich he was reunited with Minna, whom he had rashly informed about his affair with Jessie. The atmosphere in the Wagner home sank to a new low.

Bright Sounds, Dark Thoughts

CD 1 track 2
CD 2 track 2–3

www.naxosbooks.com

Website

www.naxosbooks.com

There was better news from Weimar: the indefatigable Liszt arranged and conducted the first performance of **Lohengrin** at the Court Theatre. While it was hardly a success on the scale of *Rienzi* it attracted a fair amount of interest; no doubt Wagner's political notoriety made him all the more glamorous in some quarters. When the opera was published in Leipzig in 1852, Wagner included a handsome tribute to Liszt at the beginning of the score:

> *My dear Liszt! It was you who awakened the mute lines of this score to bright-sounding life. Without your rare love for me, my work would still be lying in total silence – perhaps forgotten even by me – in some desk drawer at home. No one's ear would have perceived the music that stirred my heart and delighted my imagination when, with nothing less than a live production constantly in mind, I committed the opera to paper almost five years ago. The beautiful deed*

Franz Liszt in Munich, 1858

performed by your friendly enthusiasm, finally transforming my intentions into a real deed as well, has won me many new friends.

Then comes a sign that Wagner's hopes for the future, artistically as well as politically, are beginning to admit a note of realism:

Although the hope of seeing my work communicated to a wider audience in spirited performances is very faint – because even the most fervent enthusiasm of my friends in this regard would be faced with a state of affairs in our public cultural life that they could at present overcome only in wishes but not in reality – nevertheless I would even now be happy if I could merely arouse such a wish in their minds. That is my purpose in publishing this score, at the head of which I place the name of that friend whose victorious energy had already been able to turn the wish aroused within him into an effective deed.

It is depressing to turn from this generous tribute to another of Wagner's literary productions from the beginning of his Zurich period: the article *Das Judenthum in Musik* ('Jewishness in Music'), which he published anonymously in a German musical paper in 1850. The article includes a thinly veiled diatribe against the unfortunate Meyerbeer, but for much of its length Wagner turns his attention from the particular to the general. Jews, says Wagner, have no 'national' culture, so the art that they produce is superficial – it has no grounding in racial 'soil' and is therefore as far removed from holy Greek art as can be imagined. Jews could be acceptable, not simply by being 'assimilated' into a vibrant national culture (as many of them were attempting to do in

Jews, says Wagner, have no 'national' culture, so the art that they produce is superficial – it has no grounding in racial 'soil.'

the Germany of the latter half of the nineteenth century) but by being purged, 'redeemed' of their 'Jewishness'. This latter notion gave Wagner a valuable let-out clause during his Bayreuth years, when several of his most impassioned supporters and musical champions were of Jewish birth. But despite that codicil (with which Wagner clearly felt he was being magnanimous) it makes horrible reading, especially when one considers the use to which such ideas were put in the century that followed.

Such racial generalizations were commonplace in the nineteenth century, and not just in Germany. The great Russian novelist Fyodor Dostoyevsky also expressed some virulently anti-Semitic opinions in his *Writer's Diary*, and he too would have been echoing the prejudices of many of his countrymen. Anti-Semitism may have been less publicly evident in Victorian Britain, but it is common to find equally repellent generalizations about the Irish in the literature of the period. None of this really excuses Wagner, however, and even in nineteenth-century Germany there were those who found his opinions excessive, even downright deplorable. Liszt, for instance, begged him to think again. Even Cosima Wagner, devoted wife of Wagner's last years, felt that there were times when his racial zeal went too far.

Even Cosima Wagner, devoted wife of Wagner's last years, felt that there were times when his racial zeal went too far.

Yet the evidence of Wagner's art, and of some of his private confidences, indicates that even within his mind the issue was always more complicated than he was prepared to admit in public – take his compassion for the alleged Jewish caricatures in the *Ring*, Alberich and Mime. Others point accusingly to Wagner's claims that the Dutchman in *Der fliegende Holländer* is based on the archetypal legendary figure of the 'Wandering Jew', doomed to wander the earth forever for mocking the crucified Christ. However, Wagner also made it abundantly clear that he identified with the Dutchman. In his last years there are hints that his unconscious – or perhaps his 'better self' – was also beginning to protest against his bigotry.

Evolution of the *Ring*

In 1850 Wagner, encouraged by Liszt, began to make sketches for his 'Siegfried' opera. At around the same time he was finishing the longest and most important of his so-called 'Zurich Essays': *Oper und Drama* ('Opera and Drama'). In the essay's climactic final section, Wagner envisages a new kind of sung melody which, instead of concentrating on vocal elegance and display, focuses on the sound and meaning of the words. A

> In 1850 Wagner, encouraged by Liszt, began to make sketches for his 'Siegfried' opera.

musical motif will thus become indelibly associated with the ideas or emotions it conveys; it can then be developed by the orchestra independently of the singers, while still carrying something of its original significance (from this arises the concept of what came to be known as the Wagnerian 'Leitmotif'). This enables the orchestra to enrich its role as 'commentator' on the action: by reminding the audience of such a motif at a crucial moment, the orchestra can also bring to mind the words and feelings first associated with it. It therefore performs a role similar to that of the 'chorus' in Ancient Greek tragedy. The result would be a new kind of opera, or 'music drama' as Wagner now called it, in which the music did not attempt to impose its own patterns and structures on the drama (as in Grand Opera), but worked with it, supporting and enhancing its emotions, images and ideas.

Wagner's working title for his Siegfried opera was *Siegfrieds Tod* ('Siegfried's Death'). But his concern at this early stage was that the telling of the Siegfried story presupposed too much knowledge of the character's background. So in 1851, with the example of Aeschylus' *Oresteia* trilogy at the back of his mind, he began to plan another opera, *Der junge Siegfried* ('The Young Siegfried'), to tell the earlier part of Siegfried's story. *Siegfrieds Tod* would be renamed *Götterdämmerung* ('Twilight of the Gods'), and would form the final part of the *Ring* cycle.

Wagner's ideas for what was to become the *Ring* were still deeply rooted in his revolutionary ideology. Like Karl Marx, Wagner was still hoping that revolution might break out again, even in France; when it did, his art would be a spearhead for cultural change. But then, in December 1851 the French president Louis Napoleon staged a *coup d'état*. This enabled him to seize dictatorship, and in 1852 he proclaimed himself Emperor of the 'Second Republic' – Napoleon III. Wagner was stunned. His first reaction was one of denial, simply refusing to accept that it had happened; but then depression set in, and his letters reveal him repeatedly dwelling on thoughts of suicide.

Still, there were encouraging developments. In February 1852 he made what would be a hugely significant new contact: the rich merchant Otto Wesendonck and his beautiful, talented and much younger wife Mathilde. At the same time Wagner's plans for the *Ring* continued to grow, becoming ever more extravagant. He saw now that the two Siegfried operas were not dramatically self-explanatory. There needed to be another opera, *Die Walküre* ('The Valkyrie'), telling not only how Siegfried came to be born and orphaned, but how Brünnhilde – the real 'hero' of the *Ring* – defied Wotan, ruler of the gods, and lost her own godlike status. Even *Walküre* was not enough. Finally Wagner decided to add the 'preliminary evening' *Das Rheingold* ('The Rhinegold'), which begins with

> Wagner's plans for the *Ring* continued to grow, becoming ever more extravagant.

a vision of the River Rhine as a kind of birthplace of all life.

There was little actual composition going on at this period: the dramatic ideas might have been taking shape, but of the music in which this stupendous project was to be embodied Wagner seems to have had only the vaguest ideas. And his concerns as to how such an extraordinary scheme could be realized on the stage must have added to his depression.

The *Ring*, however, had acquired a creative momentum of its own. In 1853, having finished the cycle of librettos – or 'poems', as he now called them – Wagner published a small edition of them, from which he then read to an invited audience in Zurich later that year. Listening to the entire *Ring* text in one sitting may not seem an enthralling prospect, but by most accounts Wagner was an electrifying reader. His former theatrical experience was a huge advantage when it came to characterising the various voices in the drama. In fact the experience was probably something like hearing Wagner's contemporary Charles Dickens reading from his own novels, events that drew large and appreciative audiences.

At around the same time Wagner moved with Minna into a new, somewhat grander apartment in Zurich, which he furnished with typical ostentation and disregard for expense. In this he was encouraged by reports of increased interest in his operas abroad, and by the reaction to four performances he had conducted of *Der Fliegende Holländer* in Zurich – though as yet he had little financially to show from them. And in May he conducted three concerts, which contained excerpts from his own operas; this was not just good publicity, but also a vital opportunity to test the effectiveness of his increasingly daring orchestration. He managed a small

> Listening to the entire *Ring* text in one sitting may not seem an enthralling prospect, but by most accounts Wagner was an electrifying reader.

amount of composition, though it was far from sensational. His Piano Sonata from 1853 was written for Mathilde Wesendonck, who was arousing Wagner's interest more and more. The sonata, however, is no masterpiece, and it pales to nothingness compared with what Mathilde was soon to inspire in him.

In the summer of 1853 there followed a momentous trip to Italy, where it seems that the music for the *Ring* began to explode into consciousness. It must be remembered that Wagner was prone to gild the lily when talking of his inspirations, and some musicologists have produced evidence casting doubt on Wagner's account; but it is so gripping that it has to be quoted. In *Mein Leben* he tells how, while staying at an inn at the town of La Spezia, near Genoa, he was lying in a state of semi-consciousness induced by a fever:

I woke with a violent start from my half-sleep, realising at once that the orchestral prelude to Das Rheingold had come to me.

I suddenly had the sensation that I was sinking into a powerful current of water. This quickly developed into a concrete musical sound: a chord of E flat major, surging endlessly in rippling broken chords. From this arose melodic figures, increasing in motion, but always based in that pure chord of E flat major... I woke with a violent start from my half-sleep, realising at once that the orchestral prelude to Das Rheingold *had come to me.*

Website

www.naxosbooks.com

Wagner's sketches for **Das Rheingold** indicate that the prelude did not in fact come to him 'at once'. One of them (reproduced in the 1980 edition of the *New Grove Dictionary of Music and Musicians*) shows ideas for the prelude, but in much more nebulous form, and apparently much shorter in length. Moreover, the running motif associated with the flowing waters of the River Rhine bears a strong resemblance to a watery theme from Mendelssohn's overture *Die schöne Melusine* ('The Fair Melusine'), written in 1834 and depicting the encounter of a knight and a mermaid. Given that the first singing voices heard in *Das Rheingold* are those of the mermaid-like Rhinemaidens, the connection is irresistible. But what Wagner stole he also transformed: the *Rheingold* Prelude has a power and breathtaking originality far beyond Mendelssohn's idea and its subsequent treatment. And even if Wagner were guilty of romanticising in his La Spezia story, it is

Mathilde Wesendonck (1828–1902) aged 32

fully possible that the basic idea came to him in a fever dream or dreams – a common source of inspiration for the Romantics.

While Wagner's creative imagination began to march forward his marital relations deteriorated still further, and Minna was now showing signs of heart trouble. His feelings for Mathilde Wesendonck grew ever stronger. She was much more the kind of woman that he felt he needed: young, beautiful, intelligent and artistic (but not so much so as to rival Wagner himself) and passionately admiring. Through this time Wagner remained on excellent terms with Mathilde's husband Otto. Indeed in 1854 Otto made the extraordinary gesture of offering to pay off Wagner's debts, which then amounted to an awe-inspiring 10,000 francs. In addition, Otto supported Wagner in other practical ways; before long he would provide him with a small house, for a very reasonable rent. Wagner was meanwhile working on the music of **Die Walküre**, the first act of which centers on the theme of forbidden love – in this case the incestuous love of brother and sister, developing under the roof of the latter's husband. But before long Wagner ran into difficulties with *Walküre*; it seems that the strain of composing the opera grew too great for him. Perhaps part of the problem was that it was all just too close to home.

CD 1
track 7–11

www.naxosbooks.com

Website

www.naxosbooks.com

'Friend Schopenhauer'

In the autumn of 1854 Wagner made one of the single most important discoveries of his life. Another Zurich friend, Georg Herwegh, introduced Wagner to the *magnum opus* of the philosopher Arthur Schopenhauer, who was beginning to enjoy long-belated fame. For Wagner, Schopenhauer's *Die Welt als Wille und Vorstellung* ('The World as Will and Representation') was a bombshell. Over the next year he read it through four times. Schopenhauer – unlike most German philosophers of the nineteenth century – was as fine a writer as he was a thinker, and this would have been part of the attraction. It was, however, Schopenhauer's vision that turned Wagner's thinking upside down – yet with it went a peculiar sense of recognition. There was so much in this book that reflected what Wagner already felt, even if he had not articulated it consciously. This may seem strange, since Schopenhauer is often presented as philosophy's great pessimist, and Wagner's revolutionary theory and talk of the future had been determinedly, if not always convincingly, optimistic. On one crucial point, though, Schopenhauer, the Young Germans and Wagner all agreed: the world as it stood was a terrible place. Injustice prevailed; mindless cruelty and pointless suffering were rife. The Young Germans had believed that the world could, indeed would, be changed. Surely the great philosopher Hegel had shown for all time that history itself was an unstoppable process of change for the better? Schopenhauer laughed that idea to scorn. If there were an underlying process it was the 'Will': the blind, naked craving for life that lay at the heart of nature – in today's less metaphysically inclined age it might be called 'the selfish gene'. For Schopenhauer there was no satisfying this craving: its attempts to fulfil itself only created more suffering – for others and, ultimately, for itself. The only way out of suffering was the path undertaken by saints of all the world's great religions: renunciation, reflecting the Will back on itself, saying 'no'. If this sounds like Buddhism, it is because Schopenhauer was a thorough student of Indian scriptures,

> For Wagner, Schopenhauer's ('The World as Will and Representation') was a bombshell. Over the next year he read it through four times.

> On one crucial point, Schopenhauer and Wagner agreed: the world as it stood was a terrible place. Injustice prevailed; mindless cruelty and pointless suffering were rife.

and the Buddha's identification of 'attachment to things' as the source of human pain rang loud bells within him, as it had come to do for Wagner. Here was another possible answer to Wagner's old yearning for personal redemption and political revolution: forget Utopia, and turn instead towards Nirvana.

There was another highly relevant message for Wagner in *Die Welt als Wille und Vorstellung.* In his Zurich essays, particularly *Das Kunstwerk der Zukunft*, Wagner had put forward his idea of an ideal synthesis of the arts, all mutually subservient: the word he used in that essay was *Gesamtkunstwerk* – the 'total / unified work of art' – though it is worth noting that this is his only recorded use of that now-famous term.

For Schopenhauer, music was supreme. Through music one could achieve an almost mystical awareness of that blind craving urge within us all and stand outside it in contemplation. Music was in itself a means towards redemption. During his childhood in Danzig (now Gdańsk), Schopenhauer had heard how a cellist returning home one night was cornered by a pack of slavering bloodhounds that had escaped from a nearby warehouse. In a kind of inspired desperation the cellist had played to them. The dogs quietened down and began to listen, and the cellist was saved. Schopenhauer was enthralled by the story – and so was Wagner. He saw that his dramatic ideals would have to change. Music would not be subservient to the other arts. It had a special role to play. 'I must confess to having arrived at a clear understanding of my own works of art through the help of another,' Wagner wrote. He may have thought that he had worked out his ideas in his earlier essays, but it was only on reading Schopenhauer that he realized

Wagner saw that his dramatic ideals would have to change. Music would not be subservient to the other arts. It had a special role to play.

what he truly believed: Schopenhauer, Wagner wrote, had 'provided me with the reasoned conceptions corresponding to my intuitive principles'.

Website

www.naxosbooks.com

CD 1
track 5

www.naxosbooks.com

Still reeling from this sensational discovery, Wagner began to conceive ideas for a new opera, **Tristan und Isolde**. This would be a tale of two lovers, their desire for one another expressed in music in which sensuous beauty would combine with aching sadness. It would be desire stripped of comforting illusions, a longing that in the end could only find fulfilment in death. Musically this would be expressed by the poignant yearning motif that opens the **Tristan Prelude**. The motif is founded on a single unresolved dissonance: a dissonance that finds its true tonal resolution only in the final bars of the opera – namely after the death of both lovers. And yet Wagner's paradoxical nature declares itself even here. Evidently he had not yet renounced hope of erotic fulfilment through his relationship with Mathilde Wesendonck: the two were spending more and more time in each other's company, despite the immediate proximity of both Otto and Minna. Some years later, in a letter to Mathilde of December 1858, Wagner said that he had to correct 'friend Schopenhauer'. There was another way 'leading to the perfect appeasement of the Will': a simpler and more direct way than Schopenhauerian renunciation, by which he meant the love that 'has its roots in sex'. But only a year after this he was writing to another woman friend: 'Longingly I turn my eyes toward the land Nirvana. Yet Nirvana always becomes Tristan again.' Wagner could be accused of simply wanting to have his cake and eat it: to cling to the comforting idea of renunciation while retaining the possibility that he might fulfil his desires after all.

The greatness of *Tristan und Isolde* lies partly in the way that Wagner explores this painful paradox to the full in his music, even if he could never satisfactorily resolve it in words. Theodor Adorno ascribed this extraordinary artistic insight to 'the neurotic's ability to contemplate his own decadence and to transcend it in an image that can withstand that all-consuming gaze'. Perhaps this can be expanded by saying that the transcendence happens, but creatively. In life Wagner could not sustain his flashes of insight (moments in which a glimpse is caught of some 'better self' working away in the hinterland of consciousness) – still less live them out in his literary writings and his personal actions. In art, however, he could hold onto them and explore them much more fully. Schopenhauer himself agreed that such a thing was possible. 'In ordinary life,' he confessed ruefully, 'one is not at all that which one is at the highest moments of production.' The saint lives the ideal; the artist only glimpses it, but is still able to embody it in his work.

> In life Wagner could not sustain his flashes of insight —still less live them out in his personal actions. In art, however, he could hold onto them and explore them much more fully.

Tackling Tradition

Growing fame was producing results. In 1855 Wagner was invited by London's Philharmonic Society to conduct eight concerts. The critics reacted with hostility to Wagner's novel style of conducting, reinforcing Wagner's growing prejudice against the critical profession. The orchestra too found it hard to adapt to Wagner's demands: he wanted contrasts emphasized and important details given time to emerge clearly, even if this meant altering the basic tempo. Wagner was inclined to blame the players' difficulties on their long experience of working under Mendelssohn:

As a huge amount of music was consumed at those concerts, but only one rehearsal allowed for each performance, I myself was often obliged to leave the orchestra to its tradition, and thereby made acquaintance with a style of execution which forcibly reminded me at any rate of Mendelssohn's dictum to myself. The thing flowed on like water from a public fountain; to attempt to check it was out of the question, and every Allegro *ended as an indisputable* Presto. *The labor of intervention was painful enough; for not until one had got the right and rightly shaped tempo, did one discover the other sins of rendering that had lain swamped beneath the deluge. For one thing, the orchestra never played else but* mezzo-forte; *neither a genuine* forte, *nor a true* piano *came about. In important cases, as far as possible, I at last insisted upon the rendering that I myself had deemed right, as also on the suitable tempo. The good fellows had nothing against it, and expressed sincere delight; to the public, too, it plainly seemed the thing: but the reporters flew into a rage, and so alarmed the committee that I once was actually asked to be so good as to scurry the second movement of Mozart's Symphony in E flat again, as one had always been accustomed to and as Mendelssohn himself had done.*

The *Ring* Strikes a Reef?

On returning to Zurich, Wagner was at last able to finish *Die Walküre*. It took him until March 1856. Still hoping for some kind of reconciliation with his homeland he made an abject plea for clemency from the Saxon King Johann, full of protestations of repentance. It was rejected. Possibly influenced by this disappointment he began sketches for an opera, *Die Sieger* ('The Victors'), based on Buddhist teaching and legend – in other words, the heroes were to be 'victors' in the Schopenhauerian, world-denying sense. This came to nothing, but in the meantime Wagner began to look again at the poems for the *Ring*. Given the changes that Schopenhauer had wrought in the composer's personal ideology, did the *Ring* text – conceived in the heady days of the 1848–9 Revolution – need to be changed too? When Wagner wrote the *Ring* poems, he was still fired by the belief that revolution could destroy the powers that enslaved human beings and condemned them to suffering. Now here was Schopenhauer arguing that suffering was inevitable, inescapable, and that only detachment from the world could bring peace – and something deep within Wagner had answered with an impassioned 'Yes!'

After some equivocation Wagner decided that changing the text of the *Ring* was not necessary. To a very large extent Schopenhauer had simply articulated what, in his deepest heart, Wagner already felt: the proof of which was there in the words he had written. If on one level the *Ring* poem could be read as an argument for revolutionary socialism, with a deeper look one could also find a powerful argument for Schopenhauerian world-renunciation. The music would under-line the newly unveiled truths revealed to Wagner by 'friend Schopenhauer'. It is simply not true to assert, as Nietzsche later did, that in 1854 the *Ring* 'struck the reef of Schopenhauer' – that the discovery of Schopenhauer threw Wagner off course, and that the music he subsequently wrote was therefore unsuited to his original purpose. Most other critics have agreed that, on the whole, Wagner's decision not to alter the poem of the *Ring* was sound – with the notable exception of George Bernard Shaw, who tried to rescue what he thought was the composer's original 'socialist' message in his famous tract *The Perfect Wagnerite*.

> When Wagner wrote the *Ring* poems, he was still fired by the belief that revolution could destroy the powers that enslaved human beings and condemned them to suffering.

'In the Hothouse'

In 1857, Wagner and Minna moved into the house that Otto Wesendock had put at their disposal, next-door to his own villa just outside Zurich. Wagner christened it 'Asyl' – 'asylum', in the original sense of a haven of peace and safety from attack. At first things went well. In Asyl, Wagner first conceived the idea for what was to be his last opera, *Parsifal*. However he soon felt compelled to break off work on *Siegfried* (the new working-title for *Der junge Siegfried*), confessing that he was beginning to feel 'bored' by the *Ring*. More truthfully, perhaps, the pressure of his growing feelings for Mathilde Wesendonck, simultaneously complicated and fanned into flame by his reading of Schopenhauer, was demanding direct artistic expression. *Tristan* was forcing its way into the foreground of his creative consciousness. As a kind of 'preparatory study' for the opera, in 1857–8 Wagner set five of Mathilde's poems to music: the cycle that came to be known as the **Wesendonck Lieder**. Mathilde may not have been a great poet, but her words drew some gorgeous music from Wagner. Two of the songs, 'Im Treibhaus' ('In the Hothouse') and 'Träume' ('Dreams'), carry the subtitle 'Study for *Tristan und Isolde*', and they ended up, transformed still more magically, in Acts II and III of the opera.

> *Tristan* was forcing its way into the foreground of his creative consciousness.

It was now clear that Wagner's passion was reciprocated. How far his and Mathilde's relationship developed physically has been a subject of some disputation among scholars. If Wagner never fully consummated his passion, that might help to account for the febrile intensity of the music he had already written for the opera; but *Tristan*'s astonishing prolongation of the exquisite pain of unresolved desire over nearly four hours of music could equally have been colored by what was about to happen. Catastrophe was waiting in the wings.

Wagner committed to paper all his thoughts and feelings about Mathilde and their relationship in a letter he entitled 'Morning Confession', which he rolled inside the sketches for the Prelude to *Tristan*. Unfortunately it was Minna who found it. She had been suspicious of Wagner and Mathilde for some while, but her rage on discovering the truth was apocalyptic. There were dreadful scenes – still more so when Otto Wesendonck was brought in on the lovers' secret.

Wagner vacillated in agony between thoughts of running away with Mathilde and genuine concern for Minna's increasingly weak heart. Then, on August 17, 1858, he brought these troubles to an end by quitting his 'asylum' for good. With an old Dresden friend and admirer, Karl Ritter (son of his Paris benefactress Julie Ritter), he set off abroad, destination as yet decided. After some desolate wandering, Wagner and Ritter settled in Venice, where Wagner set to work on Act II of *Tristan und Isolde*. He found the peace needed for his work in a deserted palace on the Grand Canal; here he was able to install the piano he had recently been given by another admirer, and devote himself to *Tristan*.

In Venice, Wagner found the peace needed for his work in a deserted palace on the Grand Canal.

In Venice, work went well; but Wagner was plagued by dysentery and an ulcer on his leg. He continued to write to Mathilde, but she returned his letters unopened and he was forced to pour out his feelings of loss and thwarted desire in a diary. In *Tristan*, especially in Act II, Wagner gives a remarkably noble and empathetic portrayal of King Marke, the betrayed husband, whose discovery of the lovers results in Tristan's desperate flight abroad. Here again Wagner the artist rises above the less admirable feelings he displayed in life, some of his remarks about Otto Wesendonck in *Mein Leben* being far from generous.

Venice, however, turned out not to be the safe haven that Wagner had hoped for. At this time the city was still part of the Austrian Empire, and when the Austrian Minister of Foreign Affairs was made aware of Wagner's presence the police were instructed to watch him. Aware of this, Wagner realized that it would be unwise to stay much longer. In March 1859 he left for Lucerne, where he completed *Tristan* in August; the achievement was astonishing, considering the opera's scale and complexity, plus the sheer effort of writing out an immense, richly detailed orchestral score. (The Eulenburg edition runs for well over 1,000 pages.)

Handwritten manuscript of the end of the Prelude to Tristan und Isolde, *enclosed with a letter to Mathilde Wesendonck*

The Eulenburg edition of *Tristan* runs for well over 1,000 pages.

There was still no sign of an amnesty in Germany, so Wagner next decided to go back to Zurich and confront the Wesendoncks again. A bizarre and staggeringly insensitive move, it nevertheless paid off. With surprising magnanimity, Otto offered financial help for Wagner to complete the *Ring*. This appears to have been too much even for Wagner's conscience, and eventually the two men settled on a business deal: Otto Wesendonck would buy the copyright on the published scores from Wagner and take the income from their sale; meanwhile Wagner would keep his earnings from public performances of the cycle.

More surprises follow: Wagner decided, against all his former judgements, to make another try for success in Paris; and on arriving there he was joined – unbelievably – by Minna. Professionally, things looked a little more promising. This time Wagner was successful in gaining introduction to the influential musical circles, and he conducted three concerts of excerpts from his operas at the beginning of 1860. They attracted a great deal of interest and the music was well received, with the notable exception of the **Tristan Prelude**. Wagner's relishing of exquisite dissonance and its long-delayed resolution was evidently too advanced for his audience. Even the great innovator Berlioz pronounced himself baffled.

Then came the wonderful news that Wagner's new friends had exerted their influence and persuaded the Paris Opéra to perform *Tannhäuser*. After such an auspicious start, Wagner must have thought that his Parisian fortunes were about to change for good.

Chapter 5

'A Light Must Show Itself'

'A Light Must Show Itself'

The beginning of 1860 brought yet another encouraging development – though in this case the pill had a bitter coating. As Wagner's international reputation continued to grow, the Saxon court realized that some kind of rapprochement would have to be reached. The terms offered by King Johann were, however, singularly ungracious. If Wagner wished to enter any of the German states, then that state would have to seek permission on his behalf from Dresden. As Johann refused to have any dealings with Wagner himself, getting authorization was a bureaucratic nightmare. Wagner did manage a brief return to German soil in August – for the first time in eleven years – but it was a very different experience from his rapturous homecoming in 1842. The fatherland showed no signs of wishing to embrace its errant son.

It was hoped that success with *Tannhäuser* would effect a turnaround. The signs were still encouraging. Wagner had managed to secure the extra rehearsal time he needed, and the strenuous advocacy of Princess Pauline Metternich, wife of the Austrian ambassador in Paris, had persuaded Napoleon III to look kindly on the opera. Princess Pauline's support, however, turned out to be a very mixed blessing, as she was regarded with intense suspicion in French aristocratic circles. (Relations between Austria and France had been poor since the 1848 Revolution.) Wagner's refusal to add a second-act ballet in *Tannhäuser*, which the management rightly considered indispensable if the opera were to please fashionable opera-going tastes, was another own goal.

Wagner did revise *Tannhäuser* for the Paris production, but the music he provided for the orgiastic **Venusberg scene** at the beginning of Act I was in his most 'modernist' Tristanesque manner, far more chromatic and ambiguous in its harmonies and opulent in its orchestral colors than the version given in Dresden in 1845. The new Venusberg music was magnificent in its frenzied erotic intensity, and the new transition from the Overture into the opera's opening scene was a triumph of musical engineering. Still, it was unlikely to appeal to conservative Parisian tastes – as Wagner should have realized after the failure of the *Tristan* Prelude earlier that year. In any case, sabotage was afoot. The young patriotic aristocrats of the Jockey Club had taken strongly against this Austrian-sponsored event. At the premiere on March 13, 1861, and at the two performances that followed, they heckled, whistled, and laughed uproariously. The press reaction was appalling. Eventually Wagner conceded defeat and *Tannhäuser* was withdrawn.

CD 2
track 7

www.naxosbooks.com

Growing Hopes

There was one unforeseen favorable consequence. Elements in the Austrian Court now began to look more kindly on Wagner. The Empress's physician, Dr Standhartner, offered Wagner the use of his house while he was on holiday. Perhaps Vienna might be the right location for the first performance of *Tristan und Isolde*, an opera which, unlike *Tannhäuser*, needed no further musical surgery. Although plans for this fell through when the principal tenor fell ill, the interest generated in *Tristan* was itself encouraging. Wagner also took particular pleasure in the ministrations of the doctor's niece, Seraphine Mauro, then the lover of the composer Peter Cornelius (not that this seems to have troubled Wagner's conscience overmuch).

He now set to work on the 'poem' of **Die Meistersinger**, picking up on the sketches he had made and then put aside in 1845. Wagner read the completed poem to an audience in Mainz in 1862, with striking success. As with *Rienzi*, some of the ideas expressed in the text appeared to echo a changing mood in the German lands. Nationalist talk was on the rise again, and although the closing pages of *Meistersinger* are a hymn to German culture, rather than its potential political or military might, that may have been too fine a distinction for some of Wagner's first audiences. The new nationalism was not without its factions: there was strong disagreement between the 'Grossdeutsch' ('Greater German') camp, who felt that German national unity must include Austria, and the 'Kleindeutsch' ('Little German') thinkers, who felt that Austria, with her non-German eastern empire, was a separate case, and that the hoped-for unified German nation was probably better off without her. But it was to be force, rather than intellectual argument, that would eventually settle the matter. It was in 1862 that Prince Otto von Bismarck became minister-president of Prussia, and a decade later Bismarck, then Chancellor of Prussia, would steamroller the unification of the non-Austrian German states that so many had hoped for. At this stage, however, Wagner's feelings about Bismarck (and Prussian militarism) were highly ambiguous, and were to remain so for some time.

Wagner found lodgings in the Rhineland town of Biebrich, near Mainz. There he was joined, for the last time, by Minna. Things were bad from the start, but when a Christmas present arrived from Mathilde Wesendonck relations plummeted: 'Ten days in hell' was Wagner's verdict in a letter to Peter Cornelius. Clearly they could no longer live together, and Wagner found a home for Minna in Dresden, where his full amnesty had been announced in March 1862. It was in Dresden that Wagner and Minna were before long to have their last meeting.

Meanwhile Wagner was finding himself increasingly surrounded by female admirers, a situation he seems to have taken advantage of in some cases, though no lasting affairs developed. There was also a significant visit from the conductor Hans von Bülow and his young wife Cosima. The von Bülows had already visited Wagner at Asyl during their honeymoon in 1857, and Wagner had briefly met Cosima, daughter of his friend and champion Liszt, during his stay at La Spezia in 1853; he seems, however, to have had little inkling that this initially withdrawn young woman was to be the great love and support of his last years. At the time it appeared to be Cosima's husband – a brilliant and influential musician and one of Wagner's devotees – whom the composer was most anxious to court. Another welcome couple were the tenor Ludwig Schnorr von Carolsfeld and his wife, the soprano Malvina Schnorr von Carolsfeld. Wagner had been enormously impressed with Ludwig's interpretation of the role of Lohengrin in a recent performance and felt that he might be the singer to create the role of Tristan – a judgement that turned out to be well founded.

Still, while Wagner's hopes continued to rise, and the cultural conditions apparently grew more favorable in Germany, his tactlessness was creating problems. Those present at Wagner's reading of the *Meistersinger* poem in Vienna had included the lion among critics Eduard Hanslick, towards whom Wagner had developed a particular animus. Hanslick correctly recognized himself in the character of the pedant and clumsy suitor Beckmesser (originally named 'Hans Lick') and stormed out. Hanslick never forgave Wagner, and his sustained journalistic campaign against the composer and his supporters was a source of much pain and misunderstanding in years to come, especially in Vienna.

For the moment, though, it did nothing to dent Wagner's hopes of triumph in the Austrian capital. In 1863 he set up home in an apartment in Penzing, just outside Vienna, and furnished it with almost ludicrous extravagance. This time there was some financial justification. Among his recent, largely successful concert tours, a visit to St Petersburg had netted him a profit of 4,000 talers. As usual, however, Wagner wildly overestimated his prospects as to future income. An uprising in Poland that year against Russian domination was brutally put down, but it made travel to Russia – and thus the hoped-for renewal of Wagner's success in St Petersburg – virtually impossible. Still he continued to throw money away. At Christmas 1863 he lavished presents on his friends. Peter Cornelius, for instance, received an expensive overcoat and dressing gown, a scarf, cravats, a cigar-case and lighter, silk handkerchiefs, gold shirt-studs, a book, engraved pen-wipers, and a meerschaum cigar-holder emblazoned with his initials. It is difficult for anyone with a sense of social grace to be comfortable with such generosity. Cornelius may have adored Wagner's music, and been enthralled, at times, by his conversation; but a diary entry from 1863 shows that he could also see past the display to the heart of the man:

Wagner! There's a leading chapter! I cannot speak at length upon that subject. I say in a word: his morality is weak and without any true basis. His whole course of life, along with

his egoistic bent, has ensnared him in ethical labyrinths. He
makes use of people for his own ends, without having any
real feelings for them, without even doing them the justice
of true devotion. Within himself he has been too intent on
making his mental greatness cover all his moral weaknesses.
I am afraid posterity will be more critical.

Cornelius nevertheless continued to show towards his friend extraordinary, self-sacrificing devotion. For all Wagner's obvious 'moral weaknesses', the spell of the man and his music was just too overpowering for those who allowed themselves to come under his influence.

A Marriage of Minds

Not surprisingly, Wagner's extravagance soon caught up with him. By March 1864 his debts had reached such a peak that he had to flee Vienna to escape arrest. 'My situation is very precarious,' he wrote to Cornelius. 'A light must show itself, someone must arise to give me vigorous help now.' His prayer was to be answered sooner than he could have hoped. Earlier in 1864, Wagner had been struck by a portrait of the newly crowned King of Bavaria, Ludwig II. He was young and beautiful, and said to be keenly and intelligently interested in the arts. Unknown to Wagner, Ludwig had already sent a court official to track him down. Comically, Wagner tried at first to dodge him, convinced he must be another debt-collector; but the official persisted, and the astonished Wagner was handed a ring and a royal portrait, with a summons to appear immediately at Ludwig's court in Munich.

> For all Wagner's obvious 'moral weaknesses', the spell of the man and his music was just too overpowering for those who allowed themselves to come under his influence.

Immediately the two men were powerfully drawn to each other. Wagner was no doubt partly influenced by Ludwig's offer to finance his projects, pay off his debts, and provide him with the kind of lodgings Wagner himself felt he deserved. At first Ludwig put Wagner up in a beautiful villa just across the lake from his castle, the Schloss Berg; then he found him a fine house in Munich, from which to direct his musical campaign in the Bavarian capital. Soon he had commissioned the Dresden architect Gottfried Semper to design a theatre worthy to house the *Ring*, and there was excited talk of setting up a music school for the performance of Wagnerian music dramas. It is equally clear, however, that Wagner was deeply impressed by his sensitive, otherworldly, and passionately admiring patron.

Like Wagner, Ludwig was given to extravagant dreams – as can still be seen in some of the fantastic fairytale castles he built in the Bavarian mountains, many of them like impossibly grand operatic sets. (The most famous, Neuschwanstein, is known across the world today as the setting for the children's film *Chitty Chitty Bang Bang*.) For such a man, supporting a project like the *Ring* would have been another glorious opportunity to give substance to artistic dreams. In the first stages of their relationship Wagner and Ludwig met every day – sometimes enthusiastically exchanging ideas, sometimes sitting together in rapt silence. Ludwig's attraction to Wagner was probably also sexual, something it seems that Wagner was unable to reciprocate (though he was remarkably tolerant of homosexuality for his time); descriptions of their relationship read like accounts of a Platonic love affair.

The female emotional support he craved had at last arrived. Some time before the Vienna debacle Wagner had realized that he was strongly drawn to Cosima von Bülow.

So – miraculously – Wagner had found the powerful, generous, immensely wealthy, and artistically sympathetic patron he had long dreamed of. There were also signs that the female emotional support he craved had at last arrived. Some time before the Vienna debacle Wagner had realized that he was strongly drawn to Cosima von Bülow. She then confessed to him that she was deeply unhappy with her husband, and that she had married him more out of pity than love. Wagner still seems to have been keeping his amorous options open, but then Cosima responded to an apparently long-standing invitation from the composer by turning up at his villa, complete with two daughters and a nursemaid. This time there is firm evidence that the lovers consummated their relationship: their daughter, Isolde, was born slightly more than nine months after Cosima's arrival.

Scandal

Inevitably there were murmurings in court circles – and soon outside the royal court. Some of the official concern about the money that Ludwig was spending on Wagner, and about the influence Wagner increasingly held at court, was legitimate. Courtly sensibilities were incensed when Wagner was heard addressing the King as 'Mein Junge' ('My lad'). Gossip soon began to spread to the topic of Wagner's private life. Cosima's presence at the Wagner villa, whether or not her husband was in attendance, was noted – as was the birth of Isolde, on April 10, 1865, significantly named after the heroine of Wagner's latest opera. Awareness of this backstage whispering must have soured Wagner's pride and pleasure in becoming a father for the first time, and at the age of fifty-two.

Hans von Bülow was still staunchly loyal, conducting the first performance of **Tristan und Isolde** at the Munich Court Theatre on June 10, 1865, with Ludwig and Malvina Schnorr von Carolsfeld in the title roles. There was some

CD 1
track 5

www.naxosbooks.com

Website

www.naxosbooks.com

Notice advertising the premiere of Tristan und Isolde, *on June 10, 1865 in Munich*

bewilderment at the music, and a little hostility in some quarters, yet many others appear to have realized the major artistic significance of this event. Tragic news then added to the aura of sensationalism around Wagner: three weeks after the premiere, Ludwig Schnorr von Carolsfeld died. The story went around that it was his superhuman struggles with the ferociously demanding role of Tristan that had killed him. True or not, it helped to create a legend that *Tristan* was unperformable. Wagner himself was badly shaken. For some while afterwards he tormented himself with thoughts that he might have caused his friend and valued champion's death.

None of this would have helped Wagner's cause at the Bavarian court. Towards the end of 1865, cabinet officials mounted a campaign against him, with support from elements in the Munich press. Wagner did not help matters by publishing an article (anonymous but unmistakable in its provenance) attacking the cabinet in terms still colored by his previous revolutionary rhetoric. In the end the court officials hostile to Wagner were able to persuade Ludwig that a public uprising was imminent. Ludwig felt that his hand had been forced, and with painful regret he published an edict banning Wagner from Bavaria. This was not by any means the end of the relationship: Ludwig was to continue to support and encourage Wagner for several years. Still, Wagner's banishment from the rewarding royal presence hit him hard – and there was worse to come. While looking for somewhere new to set up home, Wagner received news from Dresden that Minna had died.

He could not bring himself to go to Dresden for the funeral, but instead threw his efforts into a solemn burial service for his dog Pohl, also recently deceased. This may look like callousness, but it could equally be an example of what psychologists call 'displacement activity': his feelings

Tribschen –
Wagner's house in
Switzerland

about Minna being too strong and complicated to find direct expression, he sought release for them by transferring his grief and care to the dog they had both loved.

Given the bitterness of some of Minna's final comments (inferred from Wagner's letters; her own do not survive), a number of Wagnerians have given Minna a bad press – Ernest Newman termed them the 'Minnaphobes'. Wagner, however, was always grateful to her for standing by him during those difficult years in Paris.

Cosima, eventually, was able to join Wagner in Switzerland, and together they found a house called Tribschen overlooking

Lake Lucerne. Ludwig was able to get away from Bavaria in secret and paid them a visit, assuring Wagner of future help. He at least appears to have been satisfied by Wagner's explanation that Cosima was there as his secretary. This was not entirely far-fetched: Cosima had already begun to take down, at Wagner's dictation, what was eventually to become his autobiography, *Mein Leben*, as well as carefully noting his table-talk, casual observations, dreams – in fact just about anything that she thought might have significance for posterity. Others were not so easily appeased. The Munich paper *Volksbote* (*The People's Messenger*) got hold of the story and made snide innuendoes, noting that 'Madame Hans de Bülow' seemed to be spending an awful lot of time 'with her "friend" (or what?) in Lucerne'. Hans von Bülow's response was to challenge the paper's editor to a duel – a challenge which the editor simply laughed off. Wagner and Cosima both sent emphatic denials to Ludwig, full of righteous indignation, which Wagner then made the basis of an open letter to Bülow. This in itself would have been unlikely to satisfy most of the gossips; but then, fortunately for Wagner, national attention was diverted elsewhere. Old disputes about the northern territory of Schleswig-Holstein, held by Denmark until 1864, finally erupted into war between Prussia and Austria, both of which saw the area as rightfully their own.

There was much more to this conflict than a dispute over who ruled a tiny handful of small, decrepit northern duchies: the winner would be in a strong position to lay claim to the governance of a future pan-German state. Wagner, who was still suspicious of Bismarck's aims, advised Ludwig to support the Austrian cause, and Ludwig took notice. In a very short time, however, it was clear that Prussia was going to win. Bismarck's victory, which made Prussia effective ruler of all the non-Austrian German states, appears to have changed Wagner's mind – as it did for many of his liberal contemporaries. This wasn't simply a case of might making right in Wagner's mind. The more he looked at Bismarck, the more he found to admire, not least the Prussian Chancellor's anti-Papist (and particularly anti-Jesuit) views. And with Bismarck's economic reforms, Wagner must have thought that he might also incline towards political liberalization.

Shattered Dreams

Closer to home matters were about to take another turn for the worse. Malvina Schnorr von Carolsfeld suddenly turned up at Tribschen, accompanied by a girl who claimed to be receiving spirit messages from her late husband. Malvina seems to have taken an instant dislike to Cosima (probably jealousy played a part here), and when Wagner bluntly warned her off she went straight to Ludwig and denounced the couple to him. Desperately, Wagner and Cosima responded by trying to persuade the King that Malvina was mad. The ugliness of their denunciations had the opposite effect from that intended: Ludwig awoke from his delusions and realized that Wagner had been deceiving him. This wasn't the final blow to the Wagner–Ludwig idyll, but the relationship never fully recovered.

The announcement of Ludwig's engagement to his cousin early in 1867 caused a resurgence of popular feeling for the King. Emboldened, Ludwig tried to put his memories of Wagner's treachery behind him and renewed his plans for a Wagner theatre and music school. The appointment of Bülow as Ludwig's Court Kapellmeister and a promising young Wagnerian, Hans Richter, as répétiteur at the court theatre increased Wagner's hopes that the breach might be healed. Meanwhile the birth of Wagner's second child Eva on

February 17 gave him added cause for rejoicing. But the effort of forgiving Wagner was too much for Ludwig, and when the architect Semper started angrily demanding payment for his work on the planned festival theatre, the King's enthusiasm for the project evaporated.

There was one last Munich triumph for Wagner: the premiere of **Die Meistersinger** under Bülow at the court theatre on June 21, 1868 was his greatest success since *Rienzi*. However, in taking his bow from the royal box, Wagner alienated many of the more conservative elements among the audience and critics, and publicly humiliated the King. This might not have been enough to destroy Ludwig's love for Wagner's music, but when it came to Wagner the man there was little chance of the King salvaging his once-precious illusions.

A New Champion?

After the success of *Die Meistersinger* Wagner and Cosima took a holiday in Italy; then Cosima moved permanently into Tribschen with her daughters. The possibility of a divorce was discussed, but as Hans von Bülow was Catholic the process of getting an annulment was extremely complicated. This does not appear to have prevented Cosima from devoting herself to Wagner with something close to religious fervor.

In 1869 Wagner found another young male devotee— someone whom, like Ludwig, he could admire, welcome as a heaven-sent ally, and patronize all at the same time. This was the brilliant, hyper-articulate and impressively well-read Friedrich Nietzsche who, at the age of twenty-four, had just been appointed Professor of Classical Philology at Basle University. Wagner, along with a need for emotional reassurance, craved academic approval for his ideas, and this

CD 2
track 1

www.naxosbooks.com

Website

www.naxosbooks.com

Nietzsche seemed to promise. Perhaps now Wagner would stop troubling himself with attempts to express his ideas in words and leave it to someone who evidently had both the necessary intelligence and the enthusiasm. For his part, Nietzsche was thrilled to be 'taken up' by such a great artist – and a composer, too! (Nietzsche had already attempted to write music, and the extent to which he loved and valued the art was comparable to that of Schopenhauer.) It is hugely ironic that Nietzsche's name is still widely associated with the Nazis and their anti-Semitism. Nietzsche made some effort to play along with Wagner's prejudices when he was still part of the Tribschen entourage, but later he turned angrily against them, coming to see anti-Semitism as a symptom of cultural 'decadence' – a decadence that he identified as having its most pernicious (though still seductive) embodiment in Wagner's music. By the time he came to write *Der Fall Wagner* (*The Case of Wagner*, 1888), the process of demonization was complete: 'Is Wagner a human being at all? Is he not a disease?'

> In 1869 Wagner found another young male devotee – the brilliant, hyper-articulate and impressively well-read Friedrich Nietzsche

For the moment, though, Nietzsche was caught up in Wagner's visionary talk of a new kind of music drama, one that was founded in the ideals of the Ancient Greeks, and particularly their great tragedians. Nietzsche's ideas of the 'Apollonian' and 'Dionysian' (the ordering/containing spirit of the god Apollo and the instinctual/anarchic urges associated with the wine-god Dionysus), and about how the two could be integrated in great works of art, were undoubtedly influenced by Wagner. So too, in all probability, was his notion of the 'Will to Power' as the primary force of human existence. Certainly Wagner represented the strongest incarnation of this within Nietzsche's close acquaintance. Nietzsche later quipped that it was a good thing for mankind that Wagner had become a composer and not a politician, where his influence could have been markedly less beneficial.

Wagner and Nietzsche were both men of emotional extremes. Like Wagner, Nietzsche could soar like an eagle in certain moods, then fall into devastating depths. Wagner could be convinced of his role as music's man of destiny, the great hope for his nation's cultural life, but then plunge into suicidal depression when faced with rejection. Similarly, in Nietzsche's philosophical writings, long after relations with Wagner have been severed, he glorifies the *Übermensch* ('Superman') and ecstatically proclaims the coming 'Revaluation of all Values', alongside some of the bleakest one-liners in nineteenth-century philosophy. 'There is no guarantee,' he writes in *Jenseits von Gute und Böse* (*Beyond Good and Evil*), 'that the truth, when it is finally uncovered, will even turn out to be interesting.'

But Nietzsche – initially – was prepared to place his hopes in Wagner and his grand, quasi-religious synthesis of the arts in music drama. He expressed his enthusiasm in his first major work, the deliberately provocative *Die Geburt der Tragödie* (*The Birth of Tragedy*, 1872), which in its original form concluded with a rapturous hymn to Wagner as the restorer of true, 'healthy' Greek values in art and philosophy.

The *Ring* Resumed

Nietzsche was present at Tribschen when Wagner's third child, christened Siegfried, was born on June 6, 1869. The composer's elation at having a son was boundless, though one may pity Siegfried when one considers the expectations his father had of him. Cosima now steeled herself and asked her husband for a divorce. Bülow could hardly be under any illusions as to the state of their marriage; at any rate, he agreed, and the long process was set in motion.

Meanwhile Wagner – after a gap of twelve years – had begun work on the *Ring* again, picking up the score of **Siegfried** at the beginning of Act III. There are those who feel that he waited too long, and that a breach in musical style is observable at this point. Perhaps, but the new act was to contain some particularly fine music, not least the exquisite moment where Brünnhilde is awakened from her long sleep by Siegfried's kiss.

Website

www.naxosbooks.com

Wagner and his son Siegfried, 1880

Far less admirable was his decision to reprint *Das Judenthum in der Musik* that same year, a decision from which many of his friends (including, apparently, the normally adoring Cosima) tried to dissuade him. Wagner was probably reacting to rumors of Bismarck's forthcoming emancipation of the Jews, passed by law in July 1869. This was not an isolated gesture: in Austria in 1860 the Emperor Franz Joseph I had relaxed the laws that controlled where Jews were allowed to live. In republishing *Das Judenthum in der Musik*, Wagner was giving voice to objections shared by many of his countrymen; its reappearance, nevertheless, was hugely controversial.

There were signs of a partial forgiveness from Ludwig, but the King now showed more determination to have things his own way, whether Wagner liked it or not. He arranged a performance of *Das Rheingold*, the world premiere, to take place on September 22, 1869. Wagner hated the idea of the 'Preliminary Evening' being heard before the *Ring* cycle was complete. He also had justified fears about how it would fare in a relatively conventional operatic production. The costume and set designs appalled him, and he had no great confidence in the musicians either. Wagner managed to persuade Hans Richter – whom Ludwig had booked to conduct the performance – to withdraw. But even this would not deter Ludwig, whose days of bowing to Wagner's superior wisdom were over, and another conductor was found just in time. The result was not quite the fiasco Wagner anticipated, but artistically and psychologically the event was a victory for Ludwig alone.

Wagner and his patron Ludwig II, discussing Das Rheingold

Defiant, Wagner now set to work on the final instalment of the *Ring*: *Götterdämmerung*. He and Cosima also began to talk seriously about the possibility of finding another site for the 'Festival Theatre' in which he could see the cycle produced to his satisfaction – although without Ludwig's help, and with no other comparable patron in sight, it could only be a dream at this stage. Ludwig for his part continued his stubborn course, staging *Die Walküre* in June 1870. This time the production was well received, but Wagner still preferred to carry on as though it had never happened.

Ludwig soon had more serious, worldly concerns on his hands. Tension between France and Bismarck's Prussia over the long-disputed territory of Alsace-Lorraine blew up into full-scale war between the two countries. This time Bavaria threw its forces behind Bismarck – a shrewd move, as it quickly turned out. All this time, feeling against France in the German states was growing, to Wagner's evident delight. What an opportunity to enjoy vicarious revenge for his humiliations in Paris! Where before he had been happy to accept the championship of Frenchmen like the poet Charles Baudelaire (who had publicly stood up for Wagner after the *Tannhäuser* scandal), now he offended French friends by criticizing their 'objectionable' poetry and 'frivolous' music.Fortunately, the Franco-Prussian war was short-lived. It soon became clear that Bismarck's armies were bigger, better equipped, and much better trained than those of Napoleon III. After the fall of Paris in January 1871 Napoleon III's regime collapsed ingloriously; like his uncle Napoleon Bonaparte, he too was to spend his last years in exile. Bismarck was now able to assume control of all the German states outside Austrian control. Under his chancellorship, the newly united Germany announced the foundation of its own 'Second Empire' ('Reich'), with

> What an opportunity to enjoy vicarious revenge for his humiliations in Paris!

Wilhelm I of Prussia as Emperor ('Kaiser'). Privately there were some German dignitaries who had their doubts about the new empire, and about the celebrations that attended its proclamation. This is how King Ludwig's brother reported back to Munich:

> *I cannot tell you, Ludwig, how infinitely distressed I felt during that ceremony, how every fiber of my being rebelled against everything I witnessed. It was all so cold, so proud, so glittering, so ostentatious and pompous and heartless and empty. I felt oppressed and utterly dejected in that hall.*

Among the people of the new Germany, however, there was an upsurge of confidence and optimism. At the same time, in Tribschen, Wagner was moving steadily towards a cultural victory of his own.

Chapter 6

'A Safe Stronghold'

'A Safe Stronghold'

On the domestic front, there were happier events for the Wagners in the summer of 1870. On July 18 came the news that Cosima's marriage to Hans von Bülow had been legally annulled. Wagner and Cosima were married at the central Protestant church in Lucerne on August 25.

As a combined wedding and birthday present for his new wife, Wagner composed his chamber-orchestral work **Siegfried Idyll**. Based partly on themes from the newly completed *Siegfried*, it is one of Wagner's loveliest creations: serene and tender, with a joyous climax incorporating the motif associated with the call of the wood-bird in the opera. Listeners who are resistant to the *Ring* often find this 'satellite' piece surprisingly easy to like. Rather less likeable is the substantial orchestral work that Wagner composed the following year to celebrate the Prussian victory over France. **Kaisermarsch** (*Imperial March*), which makes significant use of the nationally iconic Lutheran hymn-tune 'Ein' Feste Burg' ('A Safe Stronghold'), is generally leaden and bombastic. Consciously Wagner may have felt that he was doing his patriotic duty, but the music's quality suggests that his deepest artistic instincts were disengaged. While *Siegfried Idyll* remains a concert favorite, *Kaisermarsch* is virtually forgotten – revived, if at all, only as a curiosity.

Plans for Wagner's Festival Theatre were gaining momentum. The Bavarian town of Bayreuth had already

Website

www.naxosbooks.com

Website

www.naxosbooks.com

Wagner and his second wife Cosima

been suggested as a possible location, and when Wagner made an exploratory visit in April 1871 he warmed to the place immediately. A patronage scheme was set up under the direction of an energetic young admirer, Carl Tausig, while a chain of Wagner Societies was created to raise funds from other sources. Fortunately the Bayreuth town council was also enthusiastic, and offered him a generous choice of sites, free of charge, for the new theatre. It was a shrewd move on their part, for revenue from visitors since the first staging of the *Ring* cycle in 1876 has been incalculable.

Wagner chose a location on the town's 'Green Hill', and selected a plot of land next to the palace gardens for his official residence. Ludwig was gracious enough to continue offering his support, despite the friction over the Munich performances of *Das Rheingold* and *Die Walküre*. Without his aid the project would unquestionably have foundered. On May 22, 1872 the ceremonial laying of the foundation stone took place. The weather was poor, and guests had to wade

Wagner conducting Beethoven's Ninth Symphony at Bayreuth on May 22, 1872

through mud to get to the Green Hill. Wisely, the planned open-air festivities were transferred to the old opera house (far too small to accommodate Wagnerian music dramas, with their hugely expanded orchestras and ambitious scenic demands). Still, it was a decisive step forward. Wagner's dreams, which had once seemed impossibly grandiose, were on their way to fulfilment.

Wagner now began to court Bismarck, hoping that some form of state patronage might be possible for what he saw as a vital national enterprise. Bismarck decided to keep Wagner at arm's length, and there were no offers of material help. Wagner's spirits sank. To make matters worse, rejection by the Reich coincided with a cooling in diplomatic relations with Ludwig. Then suddenly Ludwig had a spectacular change of heart. 'Our plans must not founder!' he wrote to Wagner in January 1874, offering a substantial loan. Repayment over the next few years meant that Wagner had to scrap his plans for 'democratic' ticket pricing at the Festival Theatre: he had genuinely hoped that his new opera house would not be financially exclusive. It had always been his intention to make his music dramas available to ordinary people. Now there was the danger of its becoming another resort for the privileged elite, just like the hated Paris Opéra. Wagner realized, however, that he was in no position to refuse Ludwig. He hoped that perhaps the pricing could be adjusted when the debt was paid – or maybe some kind of grant scheme established to enable the less well-off to attend.

There was one consolation: the Wagners were able to move into their new villa in April 1874. Wagner gave it the name 'Wahnfried' – which might translate as 'peace' or 'relief from illusion'. The crucial element here is the word *Wahn*, 'illusion', which directly reflects Wagner's enthusiasm for

> Wagner's dreams, which had once seemed impossibly grandiose, were on their way to fulfilment.

Schopenhauer and, through his writings, for Buddhism. In the Buddha's teachings, illusion (in the original Sanskrit, *maya*) is what binds us to the world and causes suffering. The Buddhist seeks freedom from *maya* through meditation; for Wagner and Schopenhauer such detachment could also be achieved through art, and especially through music. Reconciling this with Wagner's recent patriotic enthusiasm is not easy, but appreciating the *Wahn* concept, along with Schopenhauer's related stress on the liberating power of compassion, is crucial when it comes to understanding Wagner's last opera *Parsifal*. It also stands at the heart of Hans Sachs's great monologue at the beginning of Act III of *Die Meistersinger*, 'Wahn, Wahn! Überall Wahn!' – 'Illusion, illusion! Everywhere illusion!' – as Sachs meditates on the seemingly limitless capacity of human beings for self-deception and self-torment. Once again the vision portrayed in Wagner's art transcends what he was able to embody in his day-to-day life.

November 21, 1874 was a particularly momentous day: the score of *Götterdämmerung*, and with it the whole **Ring cycle**, was complete. It was the end of a process which, from the first sketches for *Siegfrieds Tod*, had occupied Wagner – on and off – for nearly a quarter of a century. With income from concert tours to Vienna, Budapest, and Berlin he was just able to meet the cost of assembling the cast of singers and the huge orchestra required for the *Ring*, and preliminary rehearsals began in 1875. This was behind schedule, but at least the dream was now moving audibly towards solid reality.

Finally, the premiere of the complete *Ring* cycle took place, at the newly completed Bayreuth Festival Theatre. The juggernaut had proved unstoppable after all. There were three complete cycles, the first beginning on August 13, 1876. The event attracted an impressive gathering of heads of state and artistic celebrities. The Kaiser himself was there, as was

Wagner giving a toast at the premiere of Das Rheingold *as part of the* Ring *cycle premiere at Bayreuth, August 13, 1876, surrounded by his supporters – probably Franz Liszt, Cosima Wagner, and Hans von Bülow*

Pedro II of Brazil, and Ludwig, who also attended the final rehearsals – this was to be his first meeting with Wagner in eight years. Not surprisingly, reactions to this unprecedentedly ambitious work were mixed; but even among Wagner's supporters the general feeling seems to have been that the performances were more important as an achievement than for their intrinsic artistic merit. Wagner himself was unhappy with the staging – still more so with Hans Richter's conducting: 'Richter not sure of a single tempo,' he noted in his diary, 'dismal experiences indeed!' Tempo remained a factor over which Wagner took particular concern. Interestingly he often complained that conductors took his music too slowly; those who find Wagner's later works ponderous in performance may be more in sympathy with the composer's thinking than they realize.

The Cathedral of Art

How successful was the inaugural *Ring*? Noting how Wagner continued to struggle with debt as a result of his Bayreuth enterprises, Ernest Newman wrote that, 'In the strictest sense of the words it was he [Wagner] who paid for conferring Bayreuth on a frigid and hostile German world.' Newman knew what he was talking about, and would not have made such a general observation without plenty of research to back it up. But it is equally clear that a Wagner cult had begun to grow apace.

The applause at the end of *Götterdämmerung* was tumultuous, so much so that Wagner felt he had to appear before the curtain and make a speech. Afterwards, the director of the publisher Schott, Ludwig Strecker, a man not given to excessive enthusiasm, wrote that 'An event of historical importance has taken place, and I can say "I was there".' The Kaiser himself added to the plaudits, telling Wagner personally, 'I did not believe that you would bring it about, and now the sun shines on your work.' At a banquet, the evening after the final night of the cycle, Wagner was presented with a silver laurel wreath, again to thunderous applause.

For the Marxist historian Eric Hobsbawm, Wagner was the supreme master of the new secular religion of culture, in which operas and theatres became temples for a new breed of worshipper.

> *[Wagner] had a sound understanding of this function when he constructed his cathedral at Bayreuth... where faithful*

115

pilgrims came to listen, in pious exaltation, for long hours and several days, and prohibited from the frivolities of untimely applause, to the master's Germanic neo-paganism. Sound not only in appreciating the connection between sacrifice and religious exaltation, but also in grasping the importance of the arts as bearers of the new secular religion of nationalism. For what, other than armies, could express that elusive concept of the nation better than the symbols of art...?

One visitor to the first Bayreuth Wagner Festival who would almost certainly have endorsed Hobsbawm's observations was Nietzsche, now tormented by doubts about his former idol. The sight of Wagner – the man who had once talked so inspiringly about revolutionizing art and society – courteously receiving the potentates of the new bourgeois philistine world at Wahnfried horrified him. 'The whole idle riff-raff of Europe had been brought together, and any prince who pleased could go in and out of Wagner's house as if it were a sporting event,' he fulminated. For Nietzsche it was quite simple: Wagner had sold out. He no longer wished to change the world, only to receive its tributes – and, of course, its money. Nietzsche attended a few rehearsals, but what he heard only made him feel worse. 'I have had enough of it all!' he told his sister. 'I do not even want to be at the first performance – but somewhere else, anywhere but here, where it is nothing but torment for me.'

Both of these writers had their own private agendas: Hobsbawm's was political, Nietzsche's more acutely personal. Great and painstaking chronicler as Hobsbawm undoubtedly is, his Marxist background would not incline him to look kindly on nineteenth-century nationalism – particularly not in its bourgeois incarnations – or on middle-class notions of the 'religion of culture'. Nietzsche's motivations for turning against Wagner were more complicated. On one level he may have been going through a form of delayed Oedipal conflict. Like Wagner, Nietzsche lost his father at a very early age, and he had been brought up in a predominantly female household. He may initially have felt that in Wagner he had found the father he needed, in which case his later rebellion could be seen as a characteristic stage in the process of growing up.

That in itself might have been enough, but Wagner's notorious tactlessness made things worse. Throughout his adult life Nietzsche suffered from terrible migraines. Wagner wrote to Nietzsche's doctor, suggesting that 'excessive masturbation' might be to blame (this belief was common in the nineteenth century). The doctor wrote back, breaking confidence, with the information that Nietzsche had picked up gonorrhoea from prostitutes. Somehow the contents of the correspondence leaked out and became Bayreuth gossip. When Nietzsche returned for the Bayreuth Festival in 1882 he found himself to be an object of scandal and derision. His conclusion – almost certainly unjust – was that Wagner had perpetrated an *'abysmal* treachery of revenge' for Nietzsche's defection. The venom directed against Wagner in Nietzsche's later works becomes easier to understand in light of this. Yet Nietzsche even then struggled on account of finding Wagner's scores so abominably 'seductive'. That he could still be stirred by the music, after such an excruciating public humiliation, is an eloquent testimony to its pathos and sensuous beauty.

Power Courted and Questioned

Some of Hobsbawm's and Nietzsche's criticisms of Wagner and the Bayreuth phenomenon are justified. There was always an element of the skilful theatrical manipulator about

Wagner. And yet beside that is the fact that the *Ring* contains not only music that could pierce any enemy's defenses, but also human insights that continue to amaze and move today. In public, Wagner may have been happy to court and flatter the 'Iron Chancellor' Bismarck and his Kaiser. In the *Ring*, however, there is the hauntingly complex figure of Wotan, chief of the gods – a figure whose pursuit of power clearly has a degree of noble motivation; however, the compromises he is forced to make in order to retain his hold on power bring him lower and lower. In the **final scene of Die Walküre**, as he reluctantly punishes his daughter Brünnhilde for her defiance by putting her into a magic sleep, Wotan realizes that the merely human hero who will release Brünnhilde will prove to be greater than himself, the power-enslaved god. Then there is Alberich, the dwarf who renounces love in the interests of wealth and power. The scene in which he is defeated by the gods' trickery and cast out into the world with nothing is truly disturbing, as Wagner almost certainly meant it to be. The realm of the *Ring* is a universe of immense moral complexity – and one can tie oneself in knots trying to explain how a man like Wagner could understand and express such things so vividly and subtly in his art.

There was always an element of the skilful theatrical manipulator about Wagner.

CD 1
track 7–11

www.naxosbooks.com

If Wagner had known, towards the end of 1876, that historians would praise him for his 'sound understanding' of contemporary bourgeois tastes, his reaction would probably have been one of hollow laughter. By the end of the year, the first Bayreuth Festival had left him with a debt of 148,000 marks. For Wagner this was a crushing confirmation of what he had already begun to suspect when the first *Ring* reached its culmination. 'There is no footing for me and my work in this day and age,' he had told Ludwig. In all the applause the *Ring* had drawn, there was little sign for him that his message of cultural regeneration through art had been truly grasped.

The *Ring* had originally been conceived as a challenge to bourgeois materialist values; there was still enough of the youthful idealist left in the older Wagner for him to feel that success with such a demonstrably materialistic audience would in itself be a kind of failure. Thoroughly disillusioned with both his cultural enterprise and the values of his people, he seriously considered selling the theatre and moving to America.

The plan came to nothing. Meanwhile, in an effort to reduce the debt, Wagner and Richter went to London in 1877 to give a series of concerts in the Royal Albert Hall. These were much more successful with both audiences and critics than those given on Wagner's first visit to London, twenty-two years earlier; but the receipts were poor – the total profit amounted to just £700. There was the partial compensation of being received throughout the city's intellectual circles as an international artistic celebrity, and in London at least he was less plagued by the gossip that inevitably attached itself to him at home. At some point in 1877 a Bavarian journalist got hold of letters from Wagner to his Parisian underwear supplier, full of detailed requests for delicate silk undergarments – the implication being that Wagner was into some form of cross-dressing. (So much for his being thoroughly in tune with bourgeois values: prurient innuendo always disgusted him.)

> There was still enough of the youthful idealist left in the older Wagner for him to feel that success with such a demonstrably materialistic audience would in itself be a kind of failure.

At the same time, the plans that Wagner had earlier formulated for a school to coach musicians in 'the correct manner of performing musico-dramatic works in the true German style' had to be shelved indefinitely due to lack of public interest. And at some stage in 1877, Cosima appears to have discovered an affair between Wagner and a young woman named Judith Gautier. It seems that Cosima was forgiving, while making it abundantly clear that the relationship had to end. On top of all this there were signs that Wagner's heart was playing up – small wonder that he was subject to frequent bouts of depression. A milder climate was recommended, and in his last years Wagner and his now quite large family were to spend more and more time in Italy.

Religion and Art

Two projects provided welcome distraction. The first was the writing of the poem and music for **Parsifal**, a theme he had been toying with since the years of his Zurich exile. He also put a fair amount of time and energy into producing his own journal, *Bayreuther Blätter*. In some of his contributions he returned to his old obsession with the Jews – speculating as to whether Christianity could be rescued from its connection with 'the tribal god of Israel'. Some of his thinking on that issue may well have influenced his work on *Parsifal*; but if it did, the message is far from explicit, and those who have attempted to find a racist undertone in the opera have had to work hard to identify this alleged subtext. More admirable in Wagner's writings was his fervently argued campaign against vivisection, which was then indulged in far more liberally and callously than it is today.

In 1880 Wagner wrote another essay, *Religion und Kunst* (*Religion and Art*). Some of what he writes borders on the bizarre – not least his suggestion that one of the reasons for the early 'decline' of Christianity is that Christ's followers failed to embrace vegetarianism. But there are some passages that have particular relevance for *Parsifal* – the following, for instance:

One could say that at the point when religion becomes

artificial it is for art to salvage the essence of religion by construing the mythical symbols, which religion wants us to believe to be literal truth in terms of their figurative value, so as to let us see their profound hidden truth through idealized representation. Whereas the priest is concerned only that the religious allegories should be regarded as factual truths, this is of no concern to the artist, since he presents his work frankly and openly as his invention.

The use of the ritual of the Mass in *Parsifal*, and of other Christian symbols (alongside ideas influenced more by Buddhism), is a means to the opening up of the 'hidden truth' within us. A direct route to that inner truth, freed from worldly illusion, can be found through the emotion of compassion – as crucial for Wagner

The use of the ritual of the Mass in *Parsifal*, and of other Christian symbols (alongside ideas influenced more by Buddhism), is a means to the opening up of the 'hidden truth' within us.

in *Parsifal* as it was for Schopenhauer in *Die Welt als Wille und Vorstellung*. To the man who feels compassion, said Schopenhauer, 'the veil of *maya* has become for the person who performs works of love, transparent, and deception... has left him. Himself, his will, he recognizes in every creature, and hence in the sufferer also.' It is the recognition contained in the famous Buddhist saying 'Tat tvam asi' – 'All this is you.' It is compassion that changes the infantile innocent Parsifal into the knowing, integrated adult, able to act as the Christ-like 'redeemer' for others.

While staying at the Villa d'Angri, on the Bay of Naples, Wagner was visited by a younger Russian painter named Paul von Joukovsky. Wagner was impressed by Joukovsky, and not in the least scandalized by his open homosexuality. He soon realized that this was the man to design *Parsifal*. Two trips the men undertook together confirmed his judgement. At the

Moorish Palazzo Rufalo and its sumptuous gardens, perched on the edge of a precipitous cliff at the town of Ravello, Wagner felt that he had just walked straight into a dream: here, surely, was the dwelling of Klingsor, just as he envisaged it for the second act of the new opera. His spontaneous exclamation – 'Klingsor's magic garden is found!' – can be seen on a plaque near the garden gate. Then Wagner and Joukovsky paid a visit to Siena Cathedral. Its grand pillars, exotically chequered in black and white marble, its beautiful tiled floor and its shady, spacious side chapels cried out to be the Temple of the Knights of the Grail in Acts I and III. Wagner asked Joukovsky to make sketches for possible set designs. He was delighted with the results, and they were incorporated, more or less unchanged, in *Parsifal*'s first production.

Redemption through Blood

In November 1880 Wagner gave a performance of the **Prelude to Parsifal** at the Royal Court and National Theatre in Munich, in the presence of King Ludwig. This would turn out to be their last meeting. Wagner then returned to Bayreuth, where he received perhaps the least savory visitor of his last years: Count Joseph-Arthur de Gobineau, author of the notorious *Essai sur L'inégalité des Races Humaines* (*Essay on the Inequality of the Human Races*). Wagner had nothing but praise for Gobineau's theory of Aryan racial supremacy, and for a while the Count was a regular guest at Wahnfried. Wagner eventually drew back from certain aspects of Gobineau's theories. Yes, he agreed, the non-white races were 'degenerate', but not incurably so. Gobineau, he felt, was too pessimistic. Through immersion in the superior culture – the 'blood' – they could be redeemed and acquire true culture. For confirmation, Wagner needed only to look at the number of Jewish musicians who had pledged themselves to him: Carl Tausig; the Bayreuth performance archivist Heinrich Porges; another Bayreuth protégé, Joseph Rubinstein; and the conductor Hermann Levi. These men clearly adored Wagner. In 1882 Levi wrote to his father, a rabbi, denying that his beloved 'master' was an out-and-out racist:

> Posterity will one day realize that Wagner was a great human being as well as a great artist, as indeed those close to him already know. Even his attacks on what he calls 'Judaism' in music and modern literature spring from the noblest motives. There is no petty anti-Semitism about him: that is proved by his manner towards me and Joseph Rubinstein and by his close friendship with Tausig, whom he loved dearly.

Levi might also have mentioned Wagner's earlier formative friendship with Samuel Lehrs. But – up to a point – Levi was pulling the wool over his own eyes. Evidence suggests that there was plenty of 'petty anti-Semitism' in Wagner's treatment of Levi, and of those others named, however much Wagner may have valued their services. As Barry Millington suggests, there could have been an element of self-hatred behind these men's attachment to Wagner. Here was perhaps the greatest embodiment of the German culture to which they wanted so much to belong; to be accepted by a figure as imposing as Wagner – a declared anti-Semite into the bargain – was the ultimate seal of approval for any Jew wishing to be, in the language of the time, 'assimilated'.

Compassion and Renunciation

If the relatively 'optimistic' element in Wagner's racial ideology offers a crumb of comfort, there is far more on offer in *Parsifal*. The central idea of wisdom achieved through compassion is conveyed through some of the most moving music Wagner ever created. One of the most surprising, and gratifying, pieces of information contained in Bryan Magee's invaluable *Wagner and Philosophy* is that the ideologists of the Third Reich – and by implication Hitler himself – were at the very least dubious about *Parsifal*. Quoting the historian Frederic Spotts's book *Bayreuth: A History of the Wagner Festival*, Magee tells us that in 1933 the Nazis pronounced *Parsifal* 'ideologically unacceptable'; also, 'For reasons never stated, *Parsifal* was banned throughout Germany after 1939, and Bayreuth complied.' The thought that Hitler may have preferred the bombast and inflated rhetoric of *Rienzi* to the vision of liberating compassion and quasi-Buddhist renunciation in *Parsifal* is potentially reassuring to those who feel that the latter opera's message has changed their lives for the better.

> The thought that Hitler may have preferred the bombast and inflated rhetoric of *Rienzi* to the vision of liberating compassion and quasi-Buddhist renunciation in *Parsifal* is potentially reassuring to those who feel that the latter opera's message has changed their lives for the better.

Might it have been that, in his deepest artistic self, Wagner felt his racist views to be unworthy of that vision contained in *Parsifal*? Cosima's diaries faithfully record all the dreams Wagner related to her – and for an artist who relied so much on the prompting of his unconscious this was valuable material. In later years he started to have dreams in which he was reconciled with Jews he had abused: Mendelssohn for instance or, more strikingly, Meyerbeer. It is very sad that on these occasions he does not seem to have been willing or able to understand the message. Otherwise compassion might have made him wise too, like his final hero Parsifal.

It was Hermann Levi who gave the world premiere of

Parsifal on August 26, 1882 at Bayreuth. The choice of Levi appears to have been partly forced on Wagner by King Ludwig, who offered the services of his court theatre musicians at a time when the composer was hardly able to say no. Wagner did, however, concede that Levi had done a better job than most.

By this time Wagner's heart was giving serious cause for concern. The Wagner family moved to the Palazzo Vendramin in Venice, where he was to spend his few remaining months. There he worked on a new essay, *Über das Weibliche im Menschlichen* ('On the Feminine in the Human'), which, apparently abandoning hope of a political solution to mankind's problems, returns partly to his youthful belief in human love as the 'molder of all noble races'. His earlier notion of an ideal synthesis of the arts now seems to have faded. Instead he

Wagner's funeral procession in Bayreuth

talked of writing purely orchestral symphonies.

On February 13, 1883, Wagner and Cosima had an almighty row about a young English singer called Carrie Pringle, one of the Flower Maidens in the recent *Parsifal*, who was planning a visit. Wagner returned to his desk, over which, later that afternoon, the maid found him slumped. He died shortly afterwards, Cosima remaining prostrate at his feet until well into the next day. His coffin was taken by gondola to the station, from which it was conveyed to Bayreuth, where he was interred in the garden at Wahnfried. It was, ironically, the hero's welcome on his own soil that he had always longed for.

Coming to Terms with Richard Wagner

There was voluminous praise for Wagner at that final ceremony at Wahnfried. Elsewhere, one of the most moving tributes came from Wagner's great contemporary, and rival in the opera house, Verdi: 'When I read the news yesterday, I may truly say I was crushed. Not a word more! – A great individual has gone from us, a name that will leave a powerful impression in the history of art.' Grief at the news of Wagner's death inspired Bruckner to pen a wonderful musical tribute to the man he called 'the thrice-blessed master' in the coda of the slow movement of his Seventh Symphony. No doubt there were others for whom it was easier to honor Wagner's achievement once the perplexing, infuriating, overbearing man was safely out of the way.

One of the most moving tributes came from Wagner's great contemporary, and rival in the opera house, Verdi: 'When I read the news yesterday, I may truly say I was crushed. Not a word more! – A great individual has gone from us, a name that will leave a powerful impression in the history of art.'

Others preferred to diminish or dismiss his achievement, from Debussy, who called the Wagnerian revolution 'a beautiful sunset mistaken for a dawn', to the radical American composer Charles Ives, who derided him as 'a soft-bodied sensualist-pussycat'. It might be fitting, however, to give the last word on this titanic yet problematical artist to a writer who struggled with Wagner throughout his long career, and whose writings on the subject are not only deeply perceptive but at times eerily prophetic: the novelist Thomas Mann. Mann was just eight years old when his titanic compatriot died in 1883, but only a few years later he began to fall under the spell of Wagner's music. He soon became troubled by what he was beginning to discover about the composer: 'as a thinker and personality he seemed to me suspect, as an artist irresistible.'

In July 1911, while staying at the Grand Hotel des Bains in Venice, Mann made an attempt to untangle what he thought and felt about this 'suspect' yet 'irresistible' composer in an essay entitled *Coming to Terms with Richard Wagner*. It is significant that at the same time, Mann was working on his novel *Death in Venice*. At one point in the novel, the composer–hero Aschenbach is said to be developing a 'little tract, a page and a half of choice prose', as he watches the beautiful boy Tadzio playing on the beach; there are strong indications that the subject is the same as that of Mann's essay. The use of music by Mahler in the Visconti film *Death in Venice* should not distract from the fact that it was Wagner whose 'death in Venice' would have been uppermost in Mann's mind.

Like Nietzsche, Mann struggled to make sense of the gigantic figure from whom he felt the need to distance himself, but his reasoning is much more temperate, more considered, and ultimately wiser than Nietzsche's. 'I can never forget what

I owe to Richard Wagner in terms of artistic pleasure and artistic understanding,' Mann admitted, 'no matter how far I move away from him in spirit.' Without Wagner's example as a 'great *narrative* artist', he said, he would never have been able to write his novel *Buddenbrooks*, with its epic portrayal of four generations of a North German bourgeois family. Mann saw Wagner as 'nineteenth century through and through, he is *the* representative German artist of that epoch, which will live on in the memory of mankind as great (perhaps) and ill-starred (for certain)' – an extraordinarily prophetic remark. Perhaps, Mann hoped, a new, 'healthier' classicism might be on its way: a new age from which it should be possible to contemplate Wagner's achievement with more objectivity; on that point, alas, Mann was less prophetic.

What then was the nature of his youthful adoration of Wagner, Mann wondered? Was it 'a love devoid of belief'? He was inclined to think so. Perhaps the art itself contained an element of demagoguery, full of theatrical 'cunning', of 'crafty and impish tricks'. And yet, Mann wrote:

> *whenever some chord, some evocative phrase from Wagner's work impinges all unexpected on my ear, I still start with joy... my spirit succumbs to that clever and ingenious wizardry, full of yearning and cunning.*

For all his attempts to separate himself from that 'cunning' Wagner, to consign him to the past or ridicule him, Mann had only to recall his experiences of the operas and he was flooded with emotion:

> *Wonderful hours of deep and solitary happiness amidst the theatre throng, hours filled with frissons and brief moments of bliss, with delights for the nerves and the intellect*

alike, and sudden glimpses into things of profound and

moving significance, such as only this incomparable art
can afford!

However hard one looks at the music, its paradoxical beauty
and 'profound significance' remain.

The Music

Prelude

Like his great Italian contemporary Verdi, Wagner concentrated almost all his greatest thoughts into one form: opera – or, as he was later to call it, music drama. It is there that the essence of his achievement is to be found. He did try his hand at other forms, however, especially in his earlier years, and three of these in particular might be helpful starting-points for those nervous about plunging straight into the operatic works. The youthful Symphony in C, written in 1832, at the end of his studies with Christian Gottlieb Müller, is most likely to be of interest to those who have already immersed themselves in the main body of Wagner's work. It is a much better piece than some Wagnerians have claimed: although clearly inspired by the example of Beethoven's purely orchestral symphonies, and perhaps also by Mozart's 'Jupiter' Symphony (No. 41 in C), it is not merely derivative. Still, it is far less characteristic, and a good deal less impressive than the **Faust-Ouvertüre** of 1840 (which Wagner revised repeatedly up to 1855).

Eine Faust-Ouvertüre was originally conceived as the first movement of a grand programmatic symphony – probably under the influence of hearing Berlioz's 'dramatic symphony' *Roméo et Juliette* in Paris. There is also a marked similarity between its downward-plunging *Allegro* motif and the main theme of the first movement of Beethoven's Ninth Symphony,

CD 2
track 4

www.naxosbooks.com

though Wagner's idea is singular enough to lend itself to different kinds of development. Most impressive of all, however, is the sinister figure given to the tuba, supported by double basses, at the opening (almost certainly representing the demonic Mephistopheles). The tuba had only recently appeared on the orchestral scene; most mid-nineteenth-century composers' use of it (if at all) is highly tentative, but Wagner seems to have realized its potential as a solo instrument almost at once. There is also a strong anticipation here of the music associated with the sleeping dragon in Acts I and II of *Siegfried*.

The finest of his songs are to be found in the cycle that has come to be known as the **Wesendonck Lieder**. These were composed in 1857–8 to poems by Mathilde Wesendonck, who was one of the inspirations behind Wagner's erotic masterpiece *Tristan und Isolde*. Written for voice and piano, the songs are much more frequently heard in the later version for voice and orchestra. Wagner himself only orchestrated one of the songs – the concluding *Träume* ('Dreams'), whose luscious harmonies and yearning two-note sighs were used to even more telling effect in the love duet at the heart of Act II of *Tristan*. The other four orchestrations were made by the Wagnerian conductor and friend of the composer Felix Mottl. Mottl's arrangements are more than competent, but Wagner's greater orchestral mastery is evident if Mottl's opening of the third song, *Im Treibhaus* ('In the Hothouse'), is compared to Wagner's version in the sombre introduction to Act III of *Tristan*.

The *Wesendonck* cycle is more than just a 'satellite work' to *Tristan und Isolde*. The three songs that Wagner did not rework are just as treasurable, particularly No. 4, *Schmerzen* ('Sorrows'), with its impassioned descending theme and radiant final cadence. And Wagner's understanding of and sympathy for the female voice, and his sensitivity when it came to word-setting are all wonderfully and concisely demonstrated in the *Wesendonck Lieder*. It is no wonder that this moving, often subtly shaded song cycle has remained in the concert repertoire.

Perhaps the loveliest of Wagner's non-operatic works is *Siegfried Idyll*, written after his marriage to Cosima von Bülow in 1870

Still, perhaps the loveliest of Wagner's non-operatic works is **Siegfried Idyll**, written after his marriage to Cosima von Bülow in 1870 and first performed at Tribschen on the morning of her birthday later that year. What Bryan Magee called Wagner's 'powerful drive of assertiveness' is strikingly absent. Instead the prevailing mood is one of tenderness and gentle intimacy. Wagner's joy in having found a home at last, with the woman he loves and a recently born son, radiates from this music, some of which derives from the opera *Siegfried* but here lends itself to a very different kind of treatment. For much of its length *Siegfried Idyll* is carried forward by a process of gradual melodic unfolding – closer perhaps to what Wagner had in mind for the purely orchestral symphonies he considered writing after his final opera *Parsifal*.

Siegfried Idyll begins with a sustained reflection on the phrase associated with Brünnhilde's words 'Ewig war ich, ewig bin ich' ('I always was, I always am') in Act III of *Siegfried*, except that the themes now develop according to their innate musical potential, rather than attempting to convey ideas or emotions from the opera. At the climax, the trumpet – silent for most of this chamber-like work – sounds the call of the wood-bird, whose 'words' Siegfried is magically enabled to understand in Act II of the opera. It is not necessary, however, to know about the themes' origins in *Siegfried* to appreciate this gorgeous orchestral meditation. The music speaks for itself.

The Operas

Wagner's first three completed operas – **Die Feen**, **Das Liebesverbot** and **Rienzi** – do not need much comment here. For the newcomer to Wagner, enough has been said about their backgrounds and general character in the 'Life' section of this book. As with the Symphony in C, they have more to offer to those who already know the mature operas and music dramas. Furthermore, they are so rarely performed that examining them at length is unlikely to be of much practical help to anyone just starting to explore Wagner seriously. For readers interested enough in *Rienzi* to want to sample a little of its style, the **Overture** contains two of the score's most memorable themes. For the purposes of this book, however, the best place to start is with the work in which Wagner felt he 'came of age' as a composer of German opera: *Der Fliegende Holländer*.

CD 1
track 1

www.naxosbooks.com

Website

www.naxosbooks.com

Der fliegende Holländer
('The Flying Dutchman')
Romantic Opera in Three Acts (originally in One Act)

First Performance: January 2, 1843,
Royal Saxon Court Theatre, Dresden

Announcement of
the premiere of Der
Fliegende Holländer
on January 2, 1843
in Dresden

Wagner originally conceived *Der fliegende Holländer* as a continuous, one-act opera. Partly for practical reasons he subsequently split up the action into a more conventional three-act structure. There are arguments for performing it either way, but when it is heard as a sustained drama, without intervals, its 'storm-swept' urgency is all the more compelling. In the following brief synopsis, the later division into three acts is indicated in brackets.

Synopsis

Website

www.naxosbooks.com

(Act I) The Norwegian coast. Imposing cliffs surround a sea-inlet. The mariner Daland is prevented from getting home by stormy winds. The ship's steersman sings longingly of his beloved, who is so near – and yet still so far. The storm blows up again and the Flying Dutchman's ship enters the bay. He is condemned to sail the seas endlessly until the Day of Judgement, as punishment for dealing with the devil. He meets Daland, and offers him immense wealth in exchange for his daughter's hand – perhaps she will be the woman once prophesied who, faithful to death, will release him from his curse. The materially minded Daland agrees almost at once. The wind changes, and the ships sail for home, Daland's crew joining in a chorus of rejoicing.

(Act II) Daland's house. Daland's daughter Senta is obsessed with a portrait of the doomed Dutchman. Her governess and other women, seated at their spinning wheels, tease Senta for her fixation with the picture. Senta tells in a ballad the story of the Dutchman's punishment, and startles everyone with the claim that she is the woman whose love can save him. The hunter Erik enters and tries to persuade Senta to ask Daland to allow her to marry him, but it is soon clear to him that she is transfixed by the Dutchman's portrait. He tells her of an ominous dream he has had, in which she kisses a mysterious stranger and goes with him out to sea. For Senta this is more confirmation of her destiny. Then Daland arrives with the Dutchman. Initially cautious, the Dutchman is touched by her compassion for him. If she wants to be his, he warns her, she must be prepared for great sacrifice. None of this dissuades Senta. Daland returns with a crowd of well-wishers, who celebrate the forthcoming wedding.

(Act III) A rocky bay in front of Daland's house. The sailors on Daland's ship are perplexed by the silence of the crew on the Dutchman's vessel and try to goad them into conversation. Suddenly a storm breaks and the Dutchman's crew reveal that they are all in the power of Satan. Daland's sailors flee, and Erik, witnessing it all, fears for Senta. His efforts to dissuade her from her self-appointed mission are, however, misinterpreted by the suspicious Dutchman, who feels sure that she has betrayed him. Frantically Senta tries to convince him that he is wrong. The Dutchman tells her who he is and sets sail in despair. Senta casts herself into the sea, whereupon a miracle occurs: the Dutchman's ship sinks, the sun breaks through the storm clouds, and Senta and the Dutchman, who is released from his curse, are seen rising hand-in-hand towards the heavens.

The Drama in Music

The **Overture**, which Wagner composed after he had finished the main body of the opera, is a superb introduction to *Der Fliegende Holländer* in more senses than one. Several of the opera's most important themes are first presented here; but Wagner's experience of tackling dramatic symphonic form in his *Faust-Ouvertüre* just a few years earlier helped him to create something more effective and compelling than simply an introductory medley of operatic highlights. Indeed, played on its own the Overture makes a gripping tone poem. The electrifying opening sets the scene better than any stage scenery could: against an elemental bare fifth on high wind and tremolando strings, horns call out the stark motif associated with the Dutchman, while surging figures on the lower strings conjure up the swell of an angry sea. A lull in the storm leads to the 'Redemption' theme on winds, introduced by cor anglais. That its first three notes strongly echo the opening of the prisoner Florestan's aria in Beethoven's *Fidelio* cannot be coincidence, given Wagner's great admiration for the opera and its story. Despite such reflective passages the overture sustains its momentum right through to its closing bars, where Wagner anticipates the opera's final ecstatic transformation of the 'Redemption' theme, the music heard as Senta and the Dutchman rise together heavenwards. It could be argued that presenting this music twice leaves the opera open to the charge of dramatic tautology; but nearly two hours of music are to pass before it is heard again, and its final appearance, as the culmination of a long, masterly build-up in tension during the finale, is still more stirring emotionally.

The Overture, which Wagner composed after he had finished the main body of the opera, is a superb introduction to *Der Fliegende Holländer.*

Generally speaking, the music of the opera does not disappoint after this magnificent orchestral curtain-raiser. Daland's music as he introduces the Dutchman to Senta for the first time has been criticised as foursquare and banal; on the other hand it could be seen as appropriate treatment for an unimaginative, materially minded man who fails to grasp the truth about his guest – a truth that Senta sees in an instant. At the opera's very beginning the calling-out of Daland's sailors has an electrifying effect, and their final descending three-note phrase ('Hallojo!') is imitated by two groups of horns, placed behind the scenes – like an eerie, inhuman echo of the sailors' cry springing back from the cliffs.

A little later, Wagner enters darker psychological territory with the Dutchman's aria. A vivid, anguished recitative, accompanied by murky fragments from the orchestra, leads to a sweeping, agitated *Allegro* as the Dutchman tells of his endless, lonely torture. But this 'aria' is far from being a conventional separate operatic number. It shifts in tempo, key, orchestral texture (even the time signature changes), and there is no neat ending: the aria dies away to a despairing slow chant from the Dutchman's crew and a distant flicker of his signature horn call. Wagner had not yet succeeded in escaping completely from the formal conventions of early-nineteenth-century opera, but passages like this foreshadow the mastery of seamless transition that he was to achieve in the later operas. Shortly afterwards, as the Dutchman makes himself known to Daland, violas and cellos give a still more remarkable foretaste of a key motif of the *Ring*: the lugubrious descending figure with an upward turn at the end closely resembles the motif associated with Wotan's frustration at the thwarting of his plans.

Wagner had not yet succeeded in escaping completely from the formal conventions of early-nineteenth-century opera, but passages like this foreshadow the mastery of seamless transition that he was to achieve in the later operas.

At the opening of what finally became Act II, the music for Senta's female companions seated at their spinning wheels sees Wagner in more conventional operatic mode. This section is a close relative of some of the folksy peasants' choruses and dances in Weber's *Der Freischütz* – just as the music for the supernatural elements in *Der Fliegende Holländer* shows Wagner rising to the challenge set by *Freischütz*'s spine-tingling 'Wolf's Glen' scene. Wagner, however, draws the women's spinning song carefully into the broader symphonic scheme of *Der Fliegende Holländer*. The women's opening dotted figure – to the onomatopoeic words 'Summ' und brumm' with which they encourage their wheels to turn – echoes both the horns' sharp 'snaps' that follow the opening 'Dutchman' motif of the Overture and the sailors' work-song figures ('Ho! He! He! Ja!') in the opera's first scene. Later, at the beginning of Act III, the Norwegian sailors' song-and-dance theme (Wagner's concession to the Parisian fashion for ballet sections in operas) also makes prominent use of the same motif. No immediately obvious psychological or philosophical message can be read into this particular motivic connection (this is not yet the world of the *Ring*, where such interconnections offer important insights into the characters' motivations or secret intentions). It seems instead that Wagner's main concern here was to establish a form of symphonic continuity such as he admired in Beethoven. But in this scene the ideal synthesis of musical and dramatic processes is still some way off.

In *Eine Mitteilung an meine Freunde* ('A Communication to my Friends') of 1851, Wagner talked about the integration of the themes in *Der Fliegende Holländer*. The germinal phrase was apparently the three-note falling figure (echoed in the opera's 'Redemption' theme) that Senta sings to the words 'Ach! wann wirst du' ('Ah, when will you, [pale seaman, find her whom you seek?]'):

I remember that before I began work on Der Fliegende Holländer, *I first sketched Senta's second-act ballad, composing both words and melody; in this piece I unknowingly planted the thematic seed of all the music in the opera: it was a concentrated poetic image of the whole drama, as it was in my mind's eye; and so, when I came to choose a description for the finished work I was strongly tempted to call it a 'dramatic ballad.' When I eventually came to the composition, the thematic image I had already conceived intuitively spread out over the entire drama like a complete, unbroken web.*

Wagner's claim that *Der Fliegende Holländer* represents thematically a 'complete, unbroken web', with everything stemming from one 'thematic seed' in Senta's ballad, stretches credibility; and yet Wagner's pride in what he achieved in this opera is, on the whole, justified. *Der Fliegende Holländer* is as impressive in its broad sweep as it is in its local details. Berlioz complained that Wagner relied overmuch on string tremolo effects, but that is also one of the features that gives *Der Fliegende Holländer* its distinctive 'tone'. Like all Wagner's mature operas it creates a sound-world that is entirely its own. Surrender to the drama and to its powerful atmosphere and such strictures seem hardly relevant.

Wagner's pride in what he achieved in this opera is, on the whole, justified. *Der Fliegende Holländer* is as impressive in its broad sweep as it is in its local details.

Other telling uses of leading motifs are to be found in *Der Fliegende Holländer*. As Daland first brings the Dutchman to his house, and the latter's eyes meet Senta's in a moment of deep mutual recognition, the timpani quietly tap out a constantly changing rhythm: a kind of developing variation on the dotted rhythmic figure prefigured in the overture's opening horn call. On one level it strongly anticipates the lugubrious drum-taps that introduce Siegfried's Funeral March in *Götterdämmerung*; yet in this context it registers beautifully the sense of time standing still as the Dutchman and his potential redeemer assess each other for the first time.

Later, when the two are left alone, there is a passage that looks forward to the more sophisticated use of motifs in the

Ring. Above a low *pianissimo* drumroll the Dutchman's horn call and Senta's phrase from her ballad – 'Ich sei's, die dich durch ihre Treu' erlöse' ('Mine shall be the faithful heart that saves you') – confront each other questioningly. Wagner's music becomes almost like the voice of an off-stage narrator: a voice asking, 'can it be true after all?' Similarly, as Erik implores Senta to change her mind about the Dutchman in the opera's finale, the orchestra hints at what the words do not tell us: the 'Redemption' motif sounds out plaintively, harmonically uncertain, on an unaccompanied solo oboe – could Senta be losing faith in her mission?

Such moments show how highly developed Wagner's musical–dramatic instincts were even at this relatively early stage in his career. In *Der Fliegende Holländer* it is possible to make too much of the anticipations of great things to come. Its relative shortcomings would seem unimportant if Wagner's later music dramas had not been written. As an example of an early-nineteenth-century Romantic opera it is fine enough in itself: a gripping tale, embodied in superbly vivid music, with depths of characterization that become clearer the more one gets to know it.

Tannhäuser
und der Sängerkrieg auf Wartburg
('Tannhäuser and the Song Contest
on the Wartburg')
Grand Romantic Opera in Three Acts

First Performance: October 19, 1845,
Royal Saxon Court Theatre, Dresden

Tannhäuser, which boasts much glorious music, is stylistically more advanced than its predecessor; it is also more problematic, however, and Wagner revised this opera more than any other. He was still making changes to it towards the end of his life, and there are indications that he would have continued doing so had he lived longer. Two substantially different scores are generally available. The first, published in 1860 (fifteen years after the world premiere in Dresden), is usually referred to as the 'Dresden' version; the second, first printed in 1875, incorporates the musical changes that Wagner made for the disastrous Paris performance of 1861, plus a new bridge passage linking the overture and Act I. The latter is routinely labelled the 'Paris' version. Neither label is strictly accurate from a historical point of view, but for convenience's sake they will be retained in the following synopsis and discussion of the music.

To complicate matters further, some conductors have opted for a mixture of the two scores, with varying degrees of success. None of these, however, can be said to have solved entirely the problems that Wagner was still trying to sort out when he died. In spite of this, *Tannhäuser* remains a fascinating, deeply revealing work, with a great deal more to offer the opera-goer than many more 'perfect' nineteenth-century operas.

Synopsis

Act I A cavern within the Venusberg ('Mountain of Venus'). An ecstatic pagan orgy is interrupted at its climax by the song of the Sirens. (In the 'Paris' score this bacchanal is longer and wilder, drawing in several more Ancient Greek mythological images in allegorical form; this was another concession to Parisian tastes, though Wagner's placing of this 'ballet' music at the beginning of the first act was highly unconventional – even provocative.) Eventually the figures withdraw, calm ensues, and Venus is left alone with the nobleman Tannhäuser. Sated with erotic pleasure, he begs to be released from Venus's thrall: the world of human beings, marked though it is with mortality and suffering, is drawing him away. She curses him: he may go, but death will never take him, and he will be forced to return to her. Calling on the Virgin Mary (the pure 'goddess' at the other extreme from Venus), he breaks free, and finds himself standing before the castle of the Wartburg, where a shepherd hymns the coming of spring. Hearing the singing of a procession of pilgrims, Tannhäuser kneels in prayer. The Landgrave (count or prince) appears, accompanied by knights who recognize Tannhäuser. When one of them, Wolfram, mentions the name of the Landgrave's beautiful, pure daughter Elisabeth, and tells him that she still longs for him, Tannhäuser agrees to come back with them to the Wartburg.

Act II Elisabeth is alone in the great hall of the Wartburg. Tannhäuser appears, led by Wolfram. Although they are both overjoyed to be reunited, Elisabeth is confused, and Wolfram fears that he has lost her love. The Landgrave suggests a song

> Wagner's placing of this 'ballet' music at the beginning of the first act was highly unconventional—even provocative.

contest, in which the singers will attempt to convey the truth about love. As a prize Elisabeth will give the victor whatever his heart desires. The contestants arrive with much ceremony, but Tannhäuser's competitors are only able to describe love in abstract, detached language. Tannhäuser, in contrast, sings from the heart, and when challenged by Wolfram he responds with a hymn of praise to Venus as the fount of all true love. The hearers are outraged, and several knights rush forward to kill Tannhäuser; but Elisabeth protects him, pledging her own life for his salvation. Tannhäuser is commanded to go to Rome and seek expiation for his sins. Hearing the chorus of pilgrims passing by, Tannhäuser kisses the hem of Elisabeth's robe and hurries out to join them.

Act III A substantial orchestral introduction tells the story of Tannhäuser's pilgrimage to Rome. The curtain rises on the valley below the Wartburg. Elisabeth waits in anguish for Tannhäuser's return. She offers her life to the Virgin in exchange for Tannhäuser's pardon. Wolfram entreats the evening star (an ambiguous symbol, standing perhaps for the Virgin, perhaps for Venus) to receive Elisabeth kindly as she enters heaven. Tannhäuser enters in great distress. The Pope has condemned him: 'Just as this staff in my hand can never blossom, so you can never be saved from the fires of hell.' In despair, Tannhäuser is determined to return to the Venusberg. In the Dresden version Wolfram then tells of Elisabeth's sacrifice, and Tannhäuser dies, redeemed, in Wolfram's arms. In the Paris version the final scene is longer: Venus appears to reclaim Tannhäuser, but on hearing of Elisabeth's sacrifice she vanishes, and Tannhäuser falls dying over Elisabeth's open coffin. The pilgrims enter, carrying a staff that has miraculously blossomed. The meaning is clear: Tannhäuser has found salvation. In both versions the opera ends with a chorus of praise.

The Drama in Music

Like the Overture to *Der Fliegende Holländer* the **Tannhäuser Overture** has become a concert classic, but its form and character are quite different. The noble pilgrims' chorus is heard first on wind, building to a splendid climax with cascading string figures. A much faster middle section then evokes the frenzied elation and erotic sweetness of the Venusberg. In the original Dresden version, the Overture ends with a triumphant return of the pilgrims' chorus with full orchestra; but Wagner, anxious to avoid any awkwardness in the chorus's return, changes its original 3/4 pulse to the faster four-in-a-bar of the preceding **Venusberg Music**. It makes a wonderfully seamless transition, as well as giving the reprise of the chorus the effect of a triumphant symphonic peroration. This is the form in which the overture is almost invariably heard in concert today.

Most composers would have been satisfied with that. In the years following *Tannhäuser*, however, Wagner was becoming increasingly impatient with the sectional nature of the operas fashionable during his Paris days. He had managed to blur the boundaries in *Der Fliegende Holländer* and impart a more continuously flowing, symphonic feel to seve-ral of its scenes. In this respect he went several degrees further in the Dresden version of *Tannhäuser*, but it

> Wagner was becoming increasingly impatient with the sectional nature of the operas fashionable during his Paris days. He had managed to blur the boundaries in *Der Fliegende Holländer*.

wasn't enough. 'I feel that in it I have approached my ideal with giant steps,' he wrote when the original score was nearly complete – but the use of the word 'approached' is telling. He may in fact have noticed that, when it came to the use of significant motifs and the integration of themes, *Tannhäuser* actually represents a stride or two backwards from *Der*

Poster for the

Paris premiere of

Tannhäuser *on*

March 13, 1861

Fliegende Holländer. He also told Cosima in 1882 that while *Tannhäuser* was 'consummate drama', musically there were some things that were 'insufficiently expressed'. This was after he had carried out the radical revision of the bacchanalian orgy scene at the beginning of Act I and, in a piece of extraordinary musical surgery, re-engineered the Overture so that instead of reprising the pilgrims' chorus it swept straight through into that expressively heightened and much-enlarged first scene.

The music of the 'Paris' revision is tremendously exciting, and Venus's response to Tannhäuser in the second scene is much more supple and sensuous; but it creates a troubling discrepancy. The new, expanded Venusberg section is far closer in style to *Tristan und Isolde* than *Tannhäuser* in its ripe, luscious chromaticism, sumptuous multi-layered orchestral textures, and more daring use of rising sequences to whip up tension. The original opening to Act I is rather plain in comparison (even though it must have sounded startlingly modern to its first Dresden audience in 1845); but, again, the Paris reworking sits uneasily with much of the opera's later music. And the presence of a four-note rising figure, very similar to the rising 'Desire' motif at the beginning of *Tristan*, enhances the feeling (at least for those who know the later opera) that this revised Venusberg music does not really 'belong' in *Tannhäuser*.

About the same time that he was working on *Tannhäuser*, Wagner wrote a letter in which he tried to explain how his creative ideas came to him:

> *Before starting to write a verse, or even to outline a scene, I am already intoxicated by the musical aroma of my subject. I have all the notes, all the characteristic motifs in my head, so that when the verses are ready and the scenes ordered, the opera proper is also finished for me and the detailed musical treatment is rather a calm and considered afterwork which the moment of real creation has preceded.*

This statement has been treated with suspicion by some musicologists. Wagner's sketches do not always bear out this idea that 'all the notes, all the characteristic motifs' were fully formed at the moment of artistic conception. Much depends, however, on what he means when he says that he has them 'in his head': Wagner does not say that they are fully, definitely presented to his conscious mind. He could be talking at this stage of a vaguer 'musical aroma', and would likely have related to Maurice Ravel's comment concerning his String Quartet: 'It's all finished, except for the notes.'

Whatever the case, the image of intoxicating musical aroma may help the reader to focus on the stylistic problems

149

in *Tannhäuser*. The original Dresden version may not be entirely consistent: there are passages that look backwards to a plainer, more conventional kind of operatic writing alongside bolder, more dramatically fluid and psychologically vivid music; but in general the score of the Dresden *Tannhäuser* has a reasonably consistent atmosphere. The Paris additions and reworkings audibly derive from an inhaling of a different kind of musical aroma. Many conductors cannot resist the temptation to include at least some of this unquestionably finer later music, but they do so at the risk of destroying the opera's overall credibility.

There are strong, characteristic elements in the Dresden score, apart from that magnificent overture. The grand 'March and Chorus' that introduces the song competition in Act II eventually became a popular 'number' in its own right, as did Wolfram's Act III prayer 'O du, mein holder Abendstern' ('O thou, my loveliest evening star') – a sweetly attractive melody, even if its simple 'vamping' accompaniment and regular phrase structure are more backward-looking and conventional than anything in *Der Fliegende Holländer*. Tannhäuser's song to Venus in Act I, in which he yearns to be allowed to go back to the everyday human world, is a fine tune, nobly expressive of the hero's awakening conscience; yet how effective is Wagner's reuse of it at the climax of Act II, where Tannhäuser now sings in praise of the Venus who once held him against his will. This unfortunately throws into relief the blandness of the previous entrants' offerings in the song competition. It can't be said that they are 'meant' to sound bland in contrast to Tannhäuser; if so, a composer of Wagner's stature could have achieved this more entertainingly. Much more impressive is the orchestral

> The grand 'March and Chorus' that introduces the song competition in Act II eventually became a popular 'number' in its own right.

introduction to Act III, depicting Tannhäuser's pilgrimage to Rome. Agitated string figures (like the 'cascading' accompaniment to the pilgrims' chorus in the Overture) suggest Tannhäuser's supplications, while a statuesque, hymn-like brass figure evokes the Pope's implacable response. Then poignant, minimally accompanied oboe and cello phrases eloquently convey Tannhäuser's despair.

Perhaps, though, there is a problem at the very heart of *Tannhäuser* that could never be solved musically. Wagner's disillusionment with Paris shortly before he began the opera had led to the beginning of a re-evaluation of some of his other values – particularly when it came to sexuality. He was no longer the youthful apostle of free love who had set out his manifesto provocatively in *Das Liebesverbot*. To some extent, the self-indulgence of the Venusberg, and Tannhäuser's rejection of it in favor of harder but more authentic human existence, reflects Wagner's rejection of the frivolous, conscience-less hedonism he found in Paris. But the opposition of this sensuous world with the rather pallid, self-sacrificing purity represented by Elisabeth placed Wagner – rather like Tannhäuser himself – in something of an emotional cleft stick. The story raises up Elisabeth as the ideal; but the music suggests that Wagner's heart is still largely with Venus. Ironically the Paris revisions only tipped the balance further in Venus's favor. Clearly this inner conflict required a deeper, subtler resolution. Wagner was to take a big step closer to that in his next opera.

CD 1
track 2

www.naxosbooks.com

Lohengrin
Romantic Opera in Three Acts

First Performance: August 28, 1850,
Grand Ducal Court Theatre, Weimar

Synopsis

Website

www.naxosbooks.com

Act I Brabant (now a Belgian province) in the tenth century. A field by a river outside Antwerp. King Heinrich I of Saxony has arrived to enlist support in fending off an attack from the Hungarians. Friedrich von Telramund, guardian of Elsa and Gottfried (children of the deceased Duke of Brabant), accuses Elsa of murdering her brother. Friedrich had wanted Elsa for himself, but, convinced that Elsa's heart lies elsewhere, he has married Ortrud, daughter of the Prince of Friesland. If Elsa is found guilty and executed, Friedrich will inherit the title of Duke of Brabant. Summoned by King Heinrich, Elsa tells how she has dreamed of a knight who will defend her honor. Friedrich agrees to take on her champion in mortal combat: the victor will be the one whom God favors. A swan appears, drawing a boat in which stands Lohengrin, clad in gleaming silver armor. Elsa recognizes him as the knight of her dream. He asks for her hand should he win the contest, but there is one condition: she must never ask him about his name, or where he comes from. She consents, and Lohengrin confesses his love for her. In the ensuing contest Lohengrin is the victor, but having won and vindicated Elsa he spares Friedrich's life. In the background, Ortrud, still in thrall to the pagan gods, is revealed as the true power behind Friedrich's schemes.

Act II The citadel of Antwerp. Friedrich and Ortrud brood together on the steps of the minster as the festivities for Lohengrin's victory are heard from the nearby knights' palace. Friedrich suspects that Ortrud has manipulated him and accuses her of deceiving him about Elsa's murder of her brother. Cleverly, Ortrud responds by taunting Friedrich for lack of resolve. He must prove himself by poisoning Elsa's mind against Lohengrin with accusations of sorcery. She also tells him that Lohengrin's 'magic' powers will evaporate if he loses so much as a finger. He is a sorcerer: that is why he has forbidden Elsa to enquire about his identity. Elsa appears on a balcony singing of her happiness. Ortrud cunningly arouses her pity, while sowing doubts in her mind about Lohengrin's devotion. Day breaks, and a herald announces Friedrich's banishment; Lohengrin will rule Brabant as Elsa's husband. As the wedding procession arrives, Ortrud challenges Lohengrin to reveal who he is. Friedrich then accuses him of sorcery, whispering to Elsa that he knows how to disempower Lohengrin. Lohengrin leads Elsa away, but as they mount the minster steps she is chilled by the sight of Ortrud, arm raised as though in triumph.

Act III The bridal chamber. Women sing to Elsa in the famous 'Bridal Chorus'. Elsa is still disturbed by what Ortrud and Friedrich have told her. Eventually she can stand it no more and asks Lohengrin who he really is. At this point Friedrich bursts in with four accomplices, but Elsa quickly hands Lohengrin a sword and he kills Friedrich. That danger is past, but now his marriage to Elsa is at an end. The scene changes back to the field from Act I, where Lohengrin announces that he must now leave. He tells of a faraway castle where knights guard the Holy Grail. These knights are sent into the world to defend the good, but they must leave if their identity is ever discovered. Thinking she is triumphant, Ortrud gloats: Elsa's brother Gottfried was not killed; instead Ortrud used her powers to turn him into a swan. Lohengrin falls to his knees in prayer. The white dove of the Grail appears, hovering about Lohengrin's boat, and the swan is transformed back into Gottfried – clad, like Lohengrin, in bright silver. It is Gottfried, Lohengrin reveals, who will now lead the Brabantines in battle. With a shriek, Ortrud falls to the ground, her powers defeated. As Lohengrin leaves, Elsa sinks lifeless into Gottfried's arms.

The Drama in Music

CD 1
track 2

www.naxosbooks.com

Nothing in Wagner's earlier output is preparation for the visionary intensity of the orchestral **Prelude**. Like the Overture to *Der Fliegende Holländer* it was written last, drawing on material already presented in the opera, but Wagner fuses it into what feels like a single, indivisible musical organism. In the dedicatory preface to the score, Wagner had thanked Liszt (who conducted the premiere) for bringing its 'mute lines' to 'bright-sounding life'. For anyone who can read music, however, that vital radiance can actually be seen on the printed first page. Chords of A major on full violins, four solo violins (playing ghostly harmonics), flutes and oboes, rise and fall seraphically, cross-fading into one another like slowly pulsating light sources. From these the 'Grail' motif slowly detaches itself, at first on much-divided violins then joined by Wagner's newly expanded woodwind section (cor anglais and bass clarinet in addition to the usual oboes and clarinets). For some time the textures are all high up in the treble, adding to the sense of weightlessness; but gradually the bass instruments enter, leading to a majestic full-orchestral climax: it is as though the Grail now stands fully revealed to the eyes of mortals. The splendor then fades, leading back to the quiet, ethereal opening

> Nothing in Wagner's earlier output is preparation for the visionary intensity of the orchestral **Prelude**.

sounds. Once again the Grail is hidden in light.

It is often asserted that Wagner's 'progressiveness' is shown in the way that he added ever more chromatic enrichments to his harmony until the tonal foundations – the sense of anchorage in traditional major or minor keys – began to collapse. One can see something like that happening in *Tristan und Isolde* and in parts of the *Ring* and *Parsifal*; but in the *Lohengrin* Prelude Wagner manages to convey his radiantly original vision in music which, for most of its length, is in the purest A major. Later in the opera, in the third scene of Act II, Wagner portrays daybreak with an elemental fanfare-crescendo based on just two common chords: D major, then C major. The gripping long crescendo centered on one chord that acts as the Prelude to *Das Rheingold* is powerfully foreshadowed here.

At the other extreme stands the music associated with Ortrud and her sinister powers at the beginning of Act II. Here tortuous chromaticism and dark orchestral coloring give a depth to her malignity that surpasses anything in *Der Fliegende Holländer* or *Tannhäuser*. Ortrud is a truly splendid operatic villainess, fully able to dominate a man like Friedrich. Her menacing gesture at the end of Act II is accompanied by an equally menacing musical motif. Foreshadowed at the beginning of the act, it is now blared out by trumpets and trombones – leaving one in no doubt as to Ortrud's capacity to inspire terror. It seems to have left a powerful impression on Tchaikovsky: the leading tragic motif of his own ballet *Swan Lake* bears a marked resemblance to Wagner's theme.

In spite of the power and increased subtlety with which Wagner represents Ortrud and her evil machinations, the powers of good and evil are, on the whole, better balanced in *Lohengrin* than in *Tannhäuser*. That Elsa, for instance, comes across as a far more believable, rounded character than the pallid Elisabeth is a tribute to the music with which Wagner fleshes her out. Her narration in Act I of her dream of the 'knight in shining armor' could so easily have been mawkish, but her eloquent vocal line carries us with her; and when the Grail motif from the prelude – again fabulously scored – sounds in the background, the effect is genuinely touching. This section is sometimes lifted from the opera and performed as a separate concert item, but without the long expectant hush that precedes it, a great deal of the effect is lost.

CD 2
track 3

www.naxosbooks.com

At the end of the opera, Wagner's refusal to pour musical pathos over Elsa's tragic death makes it all the more shocking. Even the famous 'Bridal Chorus' (sung at countless Anglophone weddings as 'Here comes the bride') reveals itself to be highly effective in context. After the surging elation of **Act III's orchestral introduction**, the chorus's poised simplicity is touching; in view of what is to happen in Lohengrin and Elsa's brief marriage, it carries an undertone of tragic irony.

Wagner has not yet freed himself from the conventions of Romantic opera in *Lohengrin*, although recitative and aria are less easy to distinguish than they are in parts of *Der Fliegende Holländer*. The choral prayer scene that precedes the contest between Lohengrin and Friedrich was a well-established operatic custom long before Wagner's time, but it hardly spoils the general effect. Perhaps it was less wise to end the magnificent Ortrud–Friedrich scene at the beginning of Act II with a relatively conventional revenge duet common in Grand Opera. When Verdi makes use of such a well-tried device at the end of Act II of *Otello* the effect is electrifying, partly because the music is of such high quality, but also because, for all Verdi's care in dovetailing the operatic numbers in this opera, number-structure seems still essential to his dramatic thinking. In the first scene of Act II of *Lohengrin* Wagner shows what he is capable of when such formal restraints are removed; but having made

Ortrud spellbindingly alive at the beginning of the act, Wagner then proceeds to treat her and Friedrich rather more like marionettes.

Lohengrin has one slightly more significant problem – or at least it can be a problem in a less than ideally sympathetic performance. Not only is the score almost entirely in four or two beats to a bar (King Heinrich's Act I prayer 'Mein Herr und Gott' – 'My Lord and God' – is the only passage in 3/4 in the entire opera), but the phrase structure is remarkably regular, so that much of the work is dominated by two- and four-bar phrases. In a bad rendition, therefore, *Lohengrin* can sound as foursquare as the average modern rock album – and much more ponderous. In the music dramas that follow *Lohengrin*, from *Rheingold* onwards, Wagner shows a much more fluid sense of pulse and phrase structure. When the conductor Thomas Beecham complained that *Götterdämmerung* 'goes on like a damned carthorse for five hours' he may simply have been intentionally provocative; but if he had applied the same image to *Lohengrin* it would have been harder to disagree. And yet, when it works, *Lohengrin*'s continuity of pulse – as in a vast symphony – can be mesmerising: what could be overly heavy takes on a feeling of grand inevitability, entirely suited to the opera's message.

Wagner has not yet completely resolved the tension between his spiritual and sensual impulses – the very tension that made *Tannhäuser* the divided work it is. But in presenting that inner conflict in the form of tragedy (the marriage of the heaven-sent Lohengrin and the ultimately all-too-human Elsa that remains fatally unconsummated) he has dramatized that tension, and in the process psychologically objectified it, in a new way. In comparison Tannhäuser's supposed redemption at the end of his

157

From Opera to Music Drama

After *Lohengrin* five years were to pass before Wagner began composing seriously again – possibly at the moment when, according to *Mein Leben*, the inspiration for the opening of *Das Rheingold* came to him in a kind of fever dream. In the intervening years he struggled to work out his new concept of the 'music drama': the true quasi-religious synthesis of the arts through which the transformation of society might be

A performance of Das Rheingold *at* Bayreuth

initiated. That at first half-grasped ideal was to find expression in the mighty *Ring* cycle, in which, Wagner said, 'I no longer gave a thought to Dresden or any other court theatre in the world; my sole preoccupation was to produce something that should free me, once and for all, from this irrational subservience.' Ghosts of traditional operatic forms – arias, love duets, ensembles – do occasionally flit through the pages of the *Ring* (at least they do after *Das Rheingold*), but Wagner's inspiration is no longer fettered or limited by them.

It did, however, take him a little while to achieve that freedom when it came to word-setting. *Das Rheingold* is perhaps the most 'dogmatic' of the operas in the cycle in that respect, following closely the principles that Wagner had worked out in his Zurich essays, particularly in *Oper und Drama*. One general rule was that there should be one note per syllable of each word (no spinning-out of sounds in melodic flights that blur the sense of the words), with rhythms derived from speech patterns. This kind of 'heightened recitative' can be melodic, but not to the extent that enjoyment of the sensual beauty obscures the meaning. Melodies may be developed in the orchestra, which carries something of the function of the chorus in Greek drama: commenting on the action, and on the character's thoughts and feelings, recollecting past events or foreshadowing the future. From *Die Walküre* onwards Wagner began to relax this law, to the unquestionable advantage of the vocal lines – keeping to the spirit if not the letter of his own laws. Yet this was not a case of simply reverting to older practices. Wagner's 'irrational subservience' to operatic convention was over.

To those around him, Wagner's burgeoning plans for the *Ring* must have seemed more extravagantly irrational than anything previously contemplated for the musical stage. Not only was he demanding effects that would tax even the most brilliant of set designers, but he was enlarging and enriching the orchestra in astonishing new ways. The scores for the *Ring* demand six harps, eight horns (the normal nineteenth-century maximum was four), an expanded woodwind section, and even require new brass instruments: bass trumpet, contrabass trombone and a quartet of the so-called 'Wagner tubas' (more like tenor and bass horns). A new kind of singer would also be necessary: one who was capable of understanding and expressing the spirit of Wagnerian music drama – and contending on equal terms with that elemental orchestral 'chorus'.

To dream such things in exile, with no prospect of the massive financial backing needed to bring it out, would have seemed to many like the maddest of delusions. Wagner's dreams, however, would eventually become reality. And this realized dream is not only one of the most ambitious works in the history of Western art but also, in the opinion of many, one of its greatest.

Wagner's dreams would eventually become reality. And this realized dream is not only one of the most ambitious works in the history of Western art but also, in the opinion of many, one of its greatest.

Der Ring des Nibelungen
('The Ring of the Nibelungs')
Ein Bühnenfestspiel für drei Tage und einen Vorabend
('A Stage-Festival Drama for Three Days
and a Preliminary Evening')

First Performance (Complete Cycle): August 13–17, 1876,
Festival Theatre (Festspielhaus), Bayreuth

Rooted in ancient myth, Wagner's *Ring* cycle has acquired a mythic status of its own. In an age when western classical music seems to play only a peripheral role in contemporary culture, the *Ring* is still very much 'there' in the popular imagination. References in newspapers, magazines and television programs suggest that many people are aware of its existence, even if it is only through the use of the famous 'Ride of the Valkyries' in Francis Ford Coppola's film *Apocalypse*

An original photograph of the set for the Ring *cycle at Bayreuth*

161

Now, or via the classic Bugs Bunny cartoon *What's Opera Doc?*. Comedians still joke about it, ridicule often tempered by a kind of grudging respect. A performance of the third act of *Die Walküre* by English National Opera at the Glastonbury Rock Festival was surprisingly successful. Then of course there is the wearyingly frequent use of 'bleeding chunks', such as 'Siegfried's Funeral March', in documentaries about the rise and fall of the Third Reich. Wagnerians may groan at the way in which Wagner's music is used these days; but the fact that it is used at all is significant.

> Wagnerians may groan at the way in which Wagner's music is used these days; but the fact that it is used at all is significant.

Nevertheless, there are still many widespread misapprehensions about the *Ring*. It is depressing how often one hears it discussed today as though it were some kind of fascist tract. The following plot synopses and discussion of the music aim to correct that impression, and surely the most powerful case against such a charge is Wagner's representation of Wotan, chief of the gods. While Wagner may have cheered on the advancing German armies in the Franco-Prussian War, and even hymned the new regime of Bismarck and Kaiser Wilhelm I in his bombastic **Kaisermarsch**, he was simultaneously putting the finishing touches to one of the most devastating and poignant critiques in art of the political 'will to power'. As portrayed in the *Ring*, Wotan is no straightforward evil tyrant. His pursuit of power has an element of honorable motivation. Although this pursuit of power corrupts him, it is also clear how much it costs him emotionally. Wotan comes to realize that the price of maintaining power is too high, and that in any case it is ultimately beyond him. In the end he bows to the inevitable: personal salvation is only to be achieved by giving assent to – even willing – his own downfall.

Website

www.naxosbooks.com

At the opposite extreme from Wotan stands not the hero Siegfried (whom even some Wagnerians find difficult to love) but the magnificent Brünnhilde, perhaps the greatest reincarnation in Romantic art of the legendary figure of Prometheus. In the ancient Greek myth, Prometheus, like Brünnhilde, is a demi-god who defies divine power and sides ultimately with human destiny. It is Brünnhilde's final act of self-sacrifice, in the name of love, that brings about the destruction of the old order; and then in the closing bars of the cycle Wagner's music hints that something new and better might be born from the ruins.

Another popular misconception is that, in its reworking of ancient legends, the *Ring* is itself creakily archaic: regularly recycled images of huge opera singers in horned helmets, clutching spears and yodelling Germanically, do nothing to dispel the suspicion that the *Ring* is fundamentally absurd and irrelevant. In fact Wagner's depiction of Wotan's corruption and eventual tragic failure are as relevant today as ever, while the themes of the disastrous despoiling of nature and the corrosive power of greed are possibly even more so. That said, Wagner did take some of his characters from medieval Nordic and Germanic epics; moreover, he set the texts in a versified language which in its use of sometimes complicated alliterative techniques can have an alienating effect for the modern listener. On paper, lines like Siegmund's 'Winterstürme wichen dem Wonnemond' ('Winter's storms soften to the winsome moon'), from Act I of *Die Walküre*, look like cumbersome tongue-twisters. Wagner's musical setting, however, turns them into an exquisite lyrical flight.

> The listener coming to the *Ring* for the first time often finds that a broad grasp of the plot, combined with the dramatic force, beauty and suggestive power of Wagner's music, is enough to carry the ear through long expanses of time.

The listener coming to the *Ring* for the first time often finds that a broad grasp of the plot, combined with the dramatic force, beauty and suggestive power of Wagner's music, is enough to carry the ear through long expanses of time. Indeed, when Wagner's magic works its spell, these legendarily gigantic works can seem shorter in performance than they actually are.

The first task, therefore, is to become familiar with the basic ingredients of the plots of the four music dramas. After that comes a brief discussion of some of the *Ring*'s major musical features.

Das Rheingold
('The Rhinegold')
Preliminary Evening (in Four Scenes)

Website
www.naxosbooks.com

First Performance: September 22, 1862,
Royal Court and National Theatre, Munich

Synopsis

Scene 1 The depths of the River Rhine. The Rhinemaidens circle a large rocky peak rising through the waters. The dwarf Alberich (one of the subterranean-dwelling Nibelungs) appears. The Rhinemaidens tease him seductively. Initially entranced, Alberich's feelings turn to fury when he realizes that he is being mocked. Then he catches sight of the Rhinegold, glinting amid the rocks. Innocently, the Rhinemaidens reveal that

Rhinemaidens in the 1876 Bayreuth premiere of the Ring *cycle, in a special contraption that gave the illusion of their swimming beneath the Rhine*

the man who can forge a ring from the gold will have power over the whole world, the condition being that he must first renounce love. To their horror, Alberich curses love and, seizing the gold, quickly disappears into the depths.

Scene 2 Dawn in the mountains. The sunlight illuminates a magnificent castle, Valhalla, the newly built fortress of the gods. The chief of the gods, Wotan, exults in this symbol of his eternal power and glory, but his wife, Fricka, reminds him of the price: the giants Fasolt and Fafner who built Valhalla have been promised Freia, keeper of the golden apples of eternal youth, as their reward. Freia rushes in, demanding protection from Fasolt and Fafner, but the giants remind Wotan of his contract. Loge, the god of fire, offers a solution. He tells of the ring Alberich has forged from the Rhinegold: perhaps the giants will take this in place of Freia? The giants agree, but take Freia as hostage to bind the wily Wotan to his word. Deprived of Freia and her magic apples, the gods start to age. Wotan resolves to retrieve the gold from Alberich, and sets off with Loge for the underworld realm of Nibelheim.

Scene 3 A vast underground cavern, echoing to the sound of pounding anvils. Alberich now rules Nibelheim by terror. His brother Mime has forged the Tarnhelm, a magic helmet giving the wearer the power to assume any shape at will. Alberich steals it from him and takes the form of a cloud of vapor, turning a volley of invisible whiplashes on his petrified brother. Alberich vaunts his power before the stricken Nibelungs. Then he notices Wotan and Loge. The cunning Loge flatters Alberich, and challenges him to demonstrate the Tarnhelm's power. Alberich then turns himself into an immense dragon. Pretending to be impressed, Loge then wonders if the Tarnhelm could also turn him into something tiny. Carried away with his own power, Alberich takes the form of a toad, whereupon Wotan and Loge capture him and spirit him away.

Scene 4 The mountains before Valhalla. Wotan and Loge force Alberich to part with the gold; when Alberich tries to retain the ring, Wotan takes it by force, telling Alberich he is now free to go. Having confronted Wotan tellingly with his own misdeeds, Alberich laughs grimly – 'Bin ich nun frei? Wirklich frei?' ('Am I then free? Really free?') – and curses the ring: suffering and death await those who wear it. He disappears, and the giants enter, insisting that, in order to have Freia back, Wotan must give them enough gold to cover her form. The Nibelung hoard is not quite enough, and the giants demand the ring to make up the difference. Wotan tries to keep it for himself, but then the Earth-goddess Erda appears and warns Wotan enigmatically that 'a dark day dawns for the gods' ('Ein düstrer Tag dämmert den Göttern'), commanding him to give up the ring. Wotan hesitates, then suddenly throws the ring onto the pile. With Freia now free, the gods regain their youth. But then an argument breaks out between the giants, in which Fafner kills Fasolt. Wotan realizes that Alberich's curse has claimed its first victim. Donner, the god of thunder, clears the air – literally – and there appears a giant rainbow bridge leading to Valhalla; the gods walk over it in triumph. There are dissenting voices amid the rejoicing, however. Loge muses to himself that the gods are really hastening to their end; and from the depths, the Rhinemaidens plead for the return of the gold, contrasting the purity of their primal waters with the

> Donner, the god of thunder, clears the air – literally – and there appears a giant rainbow bridge leading to Valhalla; the gods walk over it in triumph.

falsity of Valhalla's glory.

Die Walküre
('The Valkyrie')
First Day (in Three Acts)

First Performance: June 26, 1870,
Royal Court and National Theatre, Munich

Synopsis

Act I A stormy night. A house built around the trunk of a giant ash tree. We are now in the world of human beings. A man is being hunted through the forest. He throws himself before the hearth. Sieglinde, wife of the warrior Hunding, gives him water. A sense of strange affinity grows between them. Asked his name, he calls himself 'Wehwalt' ('Woeful'). Hunding returns. Hunding does not trust the stranger but, in keeping with the laws of hospitality, offers him shelter for the night. He also notices a striking similarity between the newcomer and Sieglinde. The stranger tells how, as a child, he returned home with his father only to find his mother dead and his twin sister stolen away. Since then he has been dogged by bad luck. He also tells how he rescued a woman who was to have been married against her will, slaying her brothers in the process. Since then he has been a hunted man. Hunding announces that he is one of those avenging hunters, and tells 'Woeful' to prepare himself for combat the following morning. The stranger recalls how his father promised to provide him with a sword in time of deepest need. Sieglinde returns, and shows the stranger a mysterious sword thrust deep into the trunk of the ash tree. As yet no one has had the strength to draw it out. Perhaps the stranger has been sent to save her from her own enforced marriage to Hunding. The house door swings open, revealing a beautiful spring night. The stranger sings of how spring has freed his sister, life, from the grip of winter. Sieglinde recognizes the stranger as her own brother and savior, sprung from the same Wälsung family as herself, and names him 'Siegmund'. Exultant, Siegmund wrenches the sword from the tree, naming it in turn 'Nothung' ('needful' – or 'that which comes in time of need'). Passionately the two fall into each other's arms, while Siegmund proclaims her as his sister and bride, mother of a new line of Wälsung heroes.

Act II A wild mountain pass with a high rocky ridge. Wotan – the real father of Siegmund and Sieglinde – enters with the Valkyrie Brünnhilde, favorite of his many daughters. (The Valkyries are the godlike horsewomen who bear heroes slain in battle to Valhalla.) Knowing that Hunding is pursuing Siegmund and Sieglinde, he orders Brünnhilde to ensure Siegmund's victory in the coming combat. But Wotan's wife Fricka will have none of it: as upholder of the bonds of marriage she demands that Hunding be allowed his revenge; moreover, Siegmund and Sieglinde's union is incestuous, and therefore intolerable. Siegmund is merely a pawn in Wotan's political scheme to restore the Rhinegold. Fricka further humiliates Wotan by exposing his rampant promiscuity. Wotan realizes that he is trapped, and resigns himself to the fulfilment of Erda's prophecy in *Das Rheingold* – only the end of everything will absolve the gods of guilt. Brünnhilde protests in vain. Wotan threatens her with terrible punishment should she rebel: Siegmund must die. Brünnhilde flies to Siegmund and tries to dissuade him from fighting Hunding, but Siegmund, filled with love for Sieglinde and his

> Wotan realizes that he is trapped, and resigns himself to the fulfilment of Erda's prophecy in *Das Rheingold* – only the end of everything will absolve the gods of guilt.

unborn child, ignores her. Brünnhlide resolves to defy Wotan and defend Siegmund as Hunding arrives, but Wotan shatters Siegmund's sword with his spear and Hunding kills him. With a contemptuous gesture Wotan strikes Hunding dead, then thunders off in pursuit of Brünnhilde who has carried off Sieglinde, together with the fragments of Nothung.

Act III The Valkyries are gathered on the summit of a mountain. Brünnhilde, arriving with Sieglinde, implores their help, but they are too fearful of Wotan's wrath. Sieglinde is in despair; but when Brünnhilde gives her the fragments of Nothung, and prophesies that her son Siegfried – the noblest hero the world has known ('den hehrsten Helden der Welt') – will wield it to victory, Sieglinde cries out in joy and runs off into the forest. Wotan now arrives, breathing vengeance: Brünnhilde is to be deprived of her powers and be banished from his sight. (But at heart Wotan is torn between his duty and his love and admiration for his daughter, who was after all carrying out his original intentions.) To the horror of the other Valkyries, Wotan condemns Brünnhilde to lie unprotected in a magic sleep, prey to the first man who finds her. He dismisses the Valkyries and prepares to deal with his errant daughter, but she stands her ground, protesting the purity of her intentions. Wotan's heart melts and he agrees to protect her with a magic fire, penetrable only by a hero who knows no fear. Wotan bids Brünnhilde farewell, kisses her to sleep, and summons Loge to surround her with fire.

Siegfried

Second Day (in Three Acts)

First Performance: August 16, 1876,
Festival Theatre (Festspielhaus), Bayreuth

Synopsis

Act I A cave in the forest. Alberich's brother Mime is trying to forge together the fragments of the shattered Nothung, but in vain. Mime has brought up the orphaned Siegfried in the hope that Siegfried will use the sword to kill the dragon who guards the ring, the Tarnhelm and the Rhinegold. (The dragon is in fact the giant Fafner, who has used the Tarnhelm's magic to transform himself into the treasure's fearsome guardian.) Siegfried arrives back at the cave and, refusing to believe Mime's claim to be his father, demands to know who his parents really were. Eventually Mime confesses that the baby Siegfried was handed to him by a dying woman, together with the fragments of Nothung. Overjoyed by this discovery, and filled with a burgeoning sense of his own destiny, Siegfried rushes back into the forest, commanding Mime to mend the sword. The Wanderer (Wotan in disguise) appears. If only to get rid of him, Mime agrees to a riddle contest. The loser's head shall be forfeit. The Wanderer successfully answers three questions from Mime, but Mime in turn finds he cannot answer the Wanderer's final riddle: who will mend Nothung? Wryly amused by Mime's terror, the Wanderer leaves, telling him that only the one who knows no fear will accomplish the task – it is to him that Mime's head is now forfeit. Siegfried returns, and, finding the sword still in pieces, begins to work on it himself. Clumsy though he is in comparison to the expert Mime, he succeeds, while Mime brews a poison to kill Siegfried once he has killed the dragon. The treasure will then be his. Siegfried cries out in triumph ('Nothung! Nothung! neidliches Schwert! Zum leben weckt' ich dir wieder' – 'Nothung! Nothung! Enviable sword! I have woken you to life again'), and with the finished sword cleaves the anvil in two, while Mime collapses in fright.

Act II The forest outside Fafner's cave. Night. Alberich, waiting by the cave, recognizes the Wanderer. Initially terrified, he taunts Wotan with his impotence: he cannot steal the ring as he knows the effectiveness of Alberich's curse. Wotan tells Alberich of Mime's plans, and suggests that Fafner might give up the gold to him if he knew what Mime intended. Wotan wakes the dragon, who refuses to listen and demands to be left to sleep. Laughing, Wotan tells Alberich that what will be will be, and departs. Mime arrives with Siegfried, the latter increasingly repelled by the dwarf. Mime leaves Siegfried by the spring where the dragon comes to slake his thirst. Cutting himself a reed pipe, Siegfried tries to imitate the birds' songs. Failing miserably, he blows a blast on his horn. This wakes the dragon, who emerges roaring from his cave. Siegfried plunges Nothung into the dragon's heart. Dying, Fafner realizes that Siegfried is an innocent tool of the scheming Mime, and warns the boy that Mime intends to kill him. Cleaning his hands of the dragon's blood, Siegfried inadvertently licks his fingers; the magical power of the blood enables him to understand the language of the birds, one of which tells him that the Nibelungs' treasure is now his. Mime hands Siegfried the poisoned drink, but Siegfried realizes his real intentions and kills him. The wood-bird then tells Siegfried of Brünnhilde, waiting in sleep for the hero who knows no fear to set her free. With the wood-bird leading, Siegfried sets off to find her.

Act III The foot of a rocky mountain. Wotan summons Erda. Though partially resigned to his fate, he hopes that she might tell him how the wheel of destiny might be slowed down. She is confused and cannot answer him, but advises him to look to Brünnhilde, the child she once bore him. Wotan now understands that he must effectively will his own downfall, and that of the gods, and he dismisses Erda. Siegfried enters, full of naive good cheer. He realizes that this mysterious 'Wanderer' is his father's killer. Wotan bars Siegfried's way with his spear, but Siegfried shatters the spear with his sword – the exact reverse of what happened when Wotan confronted Siegmund. Wotan surrenders and disappears in complete

Amalie Materna, the first Brünnhilde at Bayreuth in 1876

darkness. Blowing his horn-call, Siegfried walks through the fire surrounding Brünnhilde's rock, and finds her asleep. At first he thinks she is a man, but when he removes her breastplate he is filled with fear for the first time in his life. He sinks to the ground, catching Brünnhilde's lips with his own. She awakens and greets the world again. At first she is afraid of losing her proud independence, but Siegfried now comprehends their destiny: together they will defy the world and bring about the destruction of the old corrupt rule of the gods.

CD 2
track 8–10
www.naxosbooks.com

Götterdämmerung
('Twilight of the Gods')
Third Day (in Three Acts, with Prologue)

First Performance: August 17, 1876,
Festival Theatre (Festspielhaus), Bayreuth

Synopsis

Prologue The three Norns, the weavers of destiny, sit together spinning the golden rope of history. Then the rope snaps, and they realize that their knowledge is at an end, along with the rule of the gods. The sun rises and Brünnhilde and Siegfried awake. Siegfried is no longer a naive boy but a warrior ready for great deeds. Brünnhilde tells Siegfried that although she loves him she must set him free to fulfil his destiny. He gives her the ring as a token of his faithfulness, while she gives him her horse. Even in absence they will be present to each other. Siegfried sets off along the River Rhine, his travels represented by a substantial orchestral transition (Siegfried's Rhine Journey).

Website
www.naxosbooks.com

Act I The stronghold of the Gibichung clan by the Rhine, where Gunther is ruler. Gunther's half-brother is Hagen, who is also the son of Alberich. Hagen advises Gunther and his sister Gutrune that it makes political sense for each of them to be married soon. It turns out that Hagen has Siegfried in mind for Gutrune and Brünnhilde for Gunther. The Gibichungs are sceptical, but Hagen tells how he will give Siegfried a potion that will cause him to forget Brünnhilde; the fair Gutrune can then easily win Siegfried's heart. Siegfried's horn-call is heard echoing along the Rhine, and Hagen welcomes him ashore. Gutrune gives him the potion, which he drinks; he is then immediately smitten with Gutrune. Gunther talks of Brünnhilde, still protected by the magic fire. Siegfried shows no sign of recognising Brünnhilde's name, or anything about her, but he remembers that he can walk through fire and offers to woo her on Gunther's behalf, using the Tarnhelm to change his identity. Siegfried and Gunther swear blood brotherhood and set off together down the Rhine. Back on her rock, Brünnhilde is visited by fellow-Valkyrie Waltraute, who tells her of Wotan's last wish: that she return the ring to the Rhinemaidens and end the gods' torment for ever. But for Brünnhilde the ring is the symbol of Siegfried's love and she will not be parted with it. She hears Siegfried's horn sounding through the flames and prepares to welcome him; but the figure that emerges (clad in the Tarnhelm) has the appearance of Gunther. He snatches the ring from her finger and takes her to the cave. Nothung shall lie between them as witness that he woos her in the name of another man.

Act II The riverbank outside the Gibichungs' stronghold. Night. Hagen is asleep. Alberich appears in a shaft of moonlight and talks to him, while Hagen replies as though still in sleep. Will Hagen win the ring for him, Alberich asks? Hagen swears. Siegfried arrives and announces his successful wooing of Brünnhilde and tells of their imminent arrival. Hagen summons the Gibichung warriors to a wild feast in celebration. Gunther and Brünnhilde enter, the latter seemingly crushed. She is astonished to see Siegfried and mystified by his lack of recognition – still more by the news of his forthcoming marriage to Gutrune. Then she sees the ring on his finger and cries out that he has betrayed her. Uncomprehending, Siegfried swears by the point of Hagen's spear that he is guiltless. Brünnhilde then confides to Hagen Siegfried's secret: he can only be mortally wounded from behind, for he would never knowingly turn his back on an enemy. Convinced of Siegfried's treachery, Gunther now joins Brünnhilde and Hagen in dedicating himself to Siegfried's destruction. Still unknowing, Siegfried leads a fanfare heralding the wedding of the two couples.

CD 2
track 8–10

www.naxosbooks.com

Act III The banks of the Rhine. Lured away from his hunting companions, Siegfried encounters the Rhinemaidens. Initially teasing and flirtatious, they warn him of the ring's curse; but he refuses to be parted from it and leaves contemptuously. No matter, sing the Rhinemaidens: a 'proud woman' will inherit the ring today and will return it to them. Siegfried returns to the hunting party and, at Hagen's prompting, he tells them of Mime and Nothung, of how he slew the dragon, captured the Nibelungs' hoard and learned to understand the woodbird. But Hagen has slipped another potion into Siegfried's drink, and he remembers how he found Brünnhilde. At this Hagen distracts him and, to the horror of the other huntsmen, thrusts his spear into Siegfried's back. The hero's body is now borne aloft and carried back to the Gibichungs' stronghold (Siegfried's Funeral March). In the hall of the court Gutrune faints with shock when she sees Siegfried's body. Hagen gloats over his victory, then kills Gunther in a fight for possession of the ring; but as he reaches out to take it from Siegfried's finger, Siegfried's arm raises itself threateningly. Brünnhilde commands that a funeral pyre be built for Siegfried. She knows now that he was innocent of Hagen's schemes, and she understands that it is her destiny to free Wotan from his torment and bring about the downfall of the gods. She puts the ring on her finger and lights the pyre, then mounts her horse and rides into the flames: the ring will be cleansed of Alberich's curse by fire. The Rhine bursts its banks and floods into the hall. Hagen plunges in after the ring, but is dragged down by two of the Rhinemaidens, while the third, Flosshilde, holds the ring aloft in triumph. In the sky, Valhalla appears in flames. The reign of the gods is over.

The Drama in Music

Website

www.naxosbooks.com

Whether or not one accepts that the opening of *Das Rheingold* came to Wagner in a dream in the Italian town of La Spezia, the **Prelude** does seem to well up from the very depths of nature. Nothing Wagner had achieved in music before this compares to it in power and audacity. We hear a single note, E flat, deep down on the double basses. From this, rising horn-calls establish a chord of E flat major. That this 'natural' major chord stands very memorably for nature itself should surprise no one. Running figures on the strings oscillate and quicken, suggesting the flowing of the Rhine. Gradually the full orchestra enters, introducing new motifs. Underneath the watery running figures, woodwind play the horns' 'nature' chordal figure, but with extra notes 'filled in'. This motif is now definitively associated with the River Rhine. Each of these ideas has a marked character of its own, yet all are based on the same chord of E flat.

> This is the primal material from which so many of the *Ring's* leading musical motifs are born. The term used most frequently to describe this kind of significant theme, identifying a character, or conveying an idea or association, is Leitmotif.

This is the primal material from which so many of the *Ring's* leading musical motifs are born. The term used most frequently to describe this kind of significant theme, identifying a character, or conveying an idea or association, is Leitmotif – or, more correctly, in German, *Leitmotiv*. The term does not appear to have been coined by Wagner, but it has stuck fast, so much so as to have become virtually indispensable. Huge catalogues and commentaries have been compiled listing hundreds of these Leitmotifs, and for the newcomer they can make daunting reading. It is helpful to know a few of the most significant of these motifs before hearing the *Ring*, but here there is only space to outline a few of the more important ones.

Fortunately, many of these themes are clearly identified from the first with the character they represent or with a significant verbal phrase; and even if the listener doesn't always register them consciously, the mind can still make musical connections on a subliminal level – as many composers of film music have realized to their advantage. Take for instance a motif that appears for the first time towards the end of *Das Rheingold*: the slow, dignified but deeply sad rising figure associated with the Earth-goddess Erda (first heard on bassoon and tuba). This is in fact a minor-key version of the rising chordal 'River Rhine' motif from the orchestral prelude to the opera. The connection is clearly 'nature': the Earth-goddess and the Rhine as the primal source of life are two aspects of the same basic phenomenon. This connection may not be consciously registered, but on a more intuitive level it will almost certainly be felt – and that is what was most important for Wagner. He would not have wished his music to be approached with a kind of mental checklist, the motifs ticked off as they float past. Feeling the link is what matters; understanding can follow in its own time.

> Wagner would not have wished his music to be approached with a kind of mental checklist, the motifs ticked off as they float past. Feeling the link is what matters; understanding can follow in its own time.

As soon as one begins to unpick these connecting threads, more and more links reveal themselves. Shortly after Erda appears for the first time in *Das Rheingold* she delivers her enigmatic warning: 'Ein düstrer Tag dämmert den Göttern' ('A dark day dawns for the gods'). As she does so, her minor-key motif rises, then falls to the same rhythm, but with a change in harmony. This falling figure becomes a motif in its own right: 'Twilight of the Gods'. It is heard again at crucial twists in the plot. As Siegfried hurries forward to find Brünnhilde at the beginning of Act III of *Siegfried*, little knowing that he is about to have his fateful encounter with Wotan, the rising 'Erda' motif is heard, followed by the falling 'Twilight of the Gods' motif, now delivered with great speed and purpose: the wheel of destiny is turning faster. A still more telling use of this 'Twilight of the Gods' motif occurs at the high point of Act III of *Götterdämmerung*, where Hagen tries to take the ring from the dead Siegfried's finger. As Hagen lunges forward, and Siegfried's arm raises itself threateningly, a trumpet sounds the fanfare motif associated with the Rhinegold (based on the same rising chordal pattern as the 'River Rhine'), then the 'Twilight of the Gods' motif descends slowly on strings. The message is clear enough: nothing Hagen does can alter destiny, for he too is a pawn in a far greater game.

After the long, swelling E flat major crescendo that opens *Das Rheingold* we hear voices for the first time: the singing of the three Rhinemaidens. The first of the sisters, Woglinde, sings a greeting to the waters in another of Wagner's ripely alliterative lines: 'Weia! Waga! Woge du welle, walle zur Wiege!' ('Weia! Waga! Well, ye waters, lap me and lull me'). She sings it to a rocking, floating figure that now stands for the 'Rhinemaidens'. Rhythmically modified, however, it becomes the phrase that the wood-bird sings to Siegfried in Act II of *Siegfried* – at first wordlessly, then (once Siegfried has learned to understand the language of birds) telling him about the sleeping Brünnhilde. Again these different voices seem to be all part of one vast web of nature.

Another motif sung by the Rhinemaidens in the first scene of *Das Rheingold* has a much more ambiguous role to play in the drama. The three sing the word 'Rheingold' to a joyously falling two-note figure; the association with the word is all we need to grasp its meaning. Later, however, after Alberich has stolen the gold and forged the ring from it, this two-note falling figure takes on a new and very different character. Punched out by bass brass, with the first chord now a harsh dissonance, it stands for the malign power of the ring. The sound itself is menacing enough; the association with the ring makes it still more disturbing. Wagner's use of this motif to suggest the workings of evil behind the scenes is especially telling. In Act I of *Götterdämmerung*, when Siegfried and Gunther leave to find Brünnhilde, and Hagen is left alone, brooding, this dark motif in the orchestra informs the listener of the true nature of Hagen's plan far more eloquently than words could.

At the climax of *Das Rheingold*, when Alberich is tricked out of his treasure and he curses the ring, he does so with another musical phrase that will have far-reaching consequences. Over an ominous drumroll, Alberich sings the words 'Wie durch Fluch er mir geriet, verflucht sei dieser Ring' ('As by a curse the ring came to me, so now may this ring be accursed!'). Alberich's musical phrase becomes the spine-tingling motif of the 'Curse of the Ring'. A little later, after Fafner kills Fasolt and the gods look on in horrified silence, the 'Curse of the Ring' motif rises terrifyingly on trombones. The music underlines what the gods silently realize: the curse has already begun to work. Much later than that, at the beginning of the second scene of Act I of *Götterdämmerung*, Hagen welcomes Siegfried to the same motif, again supported by trombones. His words seem friendly enough: 'Heil! Siegfried, teurer Held!' ('Hail! Siegfried, beloved hero!'), but his singing of them to the 'Curse' motif gives them a sinister import that the audience can understand while Siegfried remains innocent.

Part of the Leitmotifs' force depends on their instantly recognizable character. They can, however, be transformed sometimes simply, sometimes with great subtlety. Working out what these transformations signify has been a great game for Wagnerians, and some of their suggestions can appear too ingenious for their own good. One may wonder whether Wagner really attached a defined meaning to each appearance or modified reappearance of a motif, or whether he in fact used them in a more abstract way: as a composer of a symphony might develop his basic themes simply on the basis of what they suggest musically. This is perhaps a roundabout way of saying that if you don't immediately understand why motif X appears at point Y in the drama, don't worry – it is possible that Wagner himself was not absolutely sure.

Take the motif sometimes labelled 'Redemption' or 'Redemption through Love'. It is first heard in Act III of *Die Walküre*: when Brünnhilde tells Sieglinde that she carries a future hero in her womb, the fruit of her love with her slain brother Siegmund, she cries out in reply, 'O hehrstes Wunder! Herrlichste Maid!' ('O glorious wonder! Noblest of maids!'). The soaring melody associated with this reappears at the height of Brünnhilde's climactic final scene in *Götterdämmerung* as she prepares to ride into the flames of Siegfried's funeral pyre. It then is heard at the very end of the opera, where, in Ernest Newman's words, it 'seems to spread its consoling wings over not merely the present scene but the whole stupendous drama'. There has been some argument about the precise meaning of this motif. When Sieglinde sings it, is the still-unborn Siegfried the 'glorious wonder' she hymns as redeemer, or is it Brünnhilde, the 'noble maid'? It could be, in fact, that its meaning changes, depending on the context. As Sieglinde first sings it, it expresses a sudden, extreme shift in her mood: previously despairing, the thought of the new life that she carries raises her again to the highest joy. When the motif is heard for the last time, hovering above the ruins of the Gibichungs' stronghold and the flames of Valhalla, it might represent a similar hope of new life, of something better that could be born from all this terrible destruction.

There are other places where Wagner's meaning is unequivocally, thrillingly clear. Siegfried's exuberant horn-call is one of the most instantly memorable motifs in the *Ring*. It is first heard in **Act I of Siegfried**, when the future hero makes his boisterous entrance. In Act III, when he walks through the encircling flames to find Brünnhilde, it sounds out against the harmonies associated with the god Loge and his magic fire. The two motifs clash startlingly – like the shock of seeing a human form walking through a raging inferno – and yet Siegfried's motif continues to sound on, unchanged and, by musical analogy, unharmed. Just as memorable is the starkly powerful downward-thrusting scale, presented on trombones, associated with Wotan's spear, symbol of his legal authority. When Siegfried shatters the spear, just before setting foot into the magic fire for the first time, we hear the motif itself shatter, sputtered out in fragments, and we know that Wotan's power is over.

Another particularly moving motivic development occurs in the **final scene of Act III of Die Walküre**. As Brünnhilde is left alone with the enraged Wotan, she lies in silence at his feet. In the orchestra pit, a solitary bass clarinet sounds a melancholy minor-key phrase that is taken up by bass strings and then cor anglais. This phrase poignantly accompanies Brünnhilde's pleading with Wotan, but as Wotan begins to soften, its plaintive minor mode becomes brighter major. Then, when Brünnhilde has at last melted Wotan's heart, and he makes his final, painful farewells, the same phrase rises magnificently, breaking like a great wave as Wotan's love for his errant daughter overrides his anger and reveals the depth of his own un-godlike, passionate frailty.

But perhaps the most moving moment in the whole cycle comes just before Brünnhilde puts on the ring and rides into the funeral pyre at the **end of Götterdämmerung**. As she quietly sings her parting words to the distant Wotan, awaiting his end in Valhalla ('Ruhe, ruhe, du Gott' – 'Rest now, rest now, thou god'), Wagner draws together a whole cluster of motifs, including the 'Curse' and the Rhinemaidens' 'Rhinegold'. We do not have to identify them exactly to understand Wagner's message: all things come together and are reconciled in this moment. As the noble brass motif associated with Valhalla sinks gently into D flat major (the ultimate tonal goal of the *Ring*), we know that evil is exorcised; that love has brought forgiveness, and now offers redemption and reborn hope.

CD 1
track 5
www.naxosbooks.com

Website
www.naxosbooks.com

Tristan und Isolde
('Tristan and Isolde')
Handlung ('Plot' or 'Action') in Three Acts

First Performance: June 10, 1865,
Royal Court and National Theatre, Munich

Synopsis

Act I At sea. Tristan's ship is making the crossing from Ireland to Cornwall, conveying Isolde, who is to be married against her will to the Cornish King Marke. A sailor sings longingly of the 'Irish maid' he has left behind, but Isolde interprets this as an insult to herself. She resolves to die rather than accept her fate, and seeing Tristan in the distance she enigmatically 'consecrates' him to death as well. Through her handmaid Brangäne she summons Tristan, but Tristan politely refuses. His companion Kurvenal responds by singing mockingly of how Tristan had killed Isolde's fiancé Morold. Enraged, Isolde then tells Brangäne how she had nursed Tristan back to health, but on recognising him as Morold's killer, decided to kill him. Only a tender look in his eyes prevented her from striking. Now he is repaying her by leading her captive to another man. Brangäne talks of her mother's magic potions, but then is horrified when Isolde chooses the death potion. Kurwenal announces that they are in sight of land. Tristan now appears and there is an angry confrontation. Isolde offers Tristan a drink in 'atonement' for his treachery. Knowing very well what the goblet contains, Tristan drinks to Isolde. She then seizes the cup and drinks the remains.

They both expect to die, but Brangäne has substituted a love potion. In truth its 'magic' only liberates the passion that they already feel for each other. As joyous sailors' cries announce the ship's homecoming, Isolde falls upon Tristan's breast.

Act II A summer night. King Marke's castle. A garden in front of Isolde's chamber. The sound of hunting horns is heard in the distance. Isolde waits nervously for Tristan. Brangäne is to signal – by putting out the torch by her door – when it is safe for Tristan to come; but Brangäne is suspicious of Tristan's friend Melot, who has arranged the hunting party to get the King away from home. Could this be a trap, she wonders? Impatiently Isolde rejects the suggestion, and puts out the torch herself. Blessed night will release her and her lover from the shackles of odious day, where they remain painfully separated. Brangäne is ordered to keep watch from a nearby tower. Tristan enters in a state of high excitement and the two lovers fall into each other's arms. Together they sing in praise of the liberation that night brings, and implore its blessing on their love: 'O sink hernieder, Nacht der Liebe' ('Sink down upon us, night of love'). In the distance Brangäne is heard warning of the approach of day, but the lovers ignore her. From tender intimacy their passion mounts in a rapturous crescendo, anticipating the opera's great final 'Liebestod'; but at its height Kurvenal bursts in and the dream is shattered. Melot has indeed set a trap, and Tristan must save himself. Too late: King Marke enters with the gloating Melot and the rest of the hunting party, but Marke is more sorrowful than angry: if Tristan is false, where is honor to be found? Again Tristan longs for night – now for the final night of death.

> From tender intimacy their passion mounts in a rapturous crescendo.

Melot draws his sword, but Tristan refuses to defend himself and sinks, wounded, into Kurvenal's arms.

Act III Tristan's castle on the coast of Brittany. In his absence, his estate has fallen into decay. Tristan himself lies, lifelessly, on a couch. The distant melancholy piping of a shepherd wakes Tristan. Kurvenal tells how he brought Tristan home, and that he has sent a messenger to Isolde in Cornwall. Even now she is on her way, and the shepherd will play a joyous tune as soon as her ship is sighted. Delirious, Tristan thinks that he sees the ship, then falls back in despair: he was born, he says, only for yearning and dying. Then he dreams of Isolde arriving to bring him atonement and peace. Suddenly the shepherd's fanfare is heard. Tristan tears the bandages from his wound and staggers towards Isolde, only to die in her arms as she arrives. Another ship is sighted, and King Marke arrives with his retinue and the traitor Melot. Kurvenal hurls himself upon Melot, striking him dead instantly but in attempting to fend off Marke and his men, he too is killed, falling at Tristan's feet. Brangäne tries to explain to Isolde how she has told the King about the love potion, and that he has come not only to forgive them both, but to offer Isolde to Tristan. But Isolde does not hear. Transfixed by the sight of the dead Tristan, she now longs for a deeper, mystical union in death, in the depths of the 'world-soul'. As her great Liebestod ('Love-death') broadens to its final resolution, Isolde sinks, as though transfigured, from Brangäne's arms onto the body of Tristan, while King Marke makes a sign of blessing upon the dead.

The Drama in Music

In almost any general history book on western classical music *Tristan und Isolde* is described as a milestone in the development of the art – a turning-point in the evolution of musical language, after which music would never be the same again. Undeniably, *Tristan* has been, and continues to be, enormously influential. In pushing extreme chromaticism of melody and harmony to unprecedented limits, Wagner released a vital new potential for emotional expression, and suggested equally new ways in which musical arguments could be pursued and forms constructed. It is possible that without the monumental example of *Tristan* before him, Schoenberg would never have had the courage to extend chromaticism still further, blurring the features of the familiar major and minor scales until tonality itself collapsed altogether.

Yet to portray *Tristan und Isolde* as just another staging-post, however significant, on the historical road to a long-anticipated 'atonal revolution' is to reduce it, and to underestimate its other innovatory features. For one thing, however long Wagner may postpone the resolution of the dissonance at the heart of *Tristan*'s opening 'Desire' motif, that resolution does eventually occur, gloriously, as Isolde sinks onto the body of her lover at the very end of the opera. Wagner's delaying of this momentous harmonic release does not in any way invalidate it or weaken it – quite the reverse. As the four rising semitones of the 'Desire' motif melt into the serene embrace of the final chord of B major, the effect can be like a revelation: for many listeners there is a moment of inner recognition, as though a voice from deep within has said, 'Of course!' Only once, at the climax of Act II, has this nearly four-hour-long opera hinted that B major might be its ultimate goal; and yet it feels so 'right'. To quote Schopenhauer, writing about the resolution of discord at the

> As the four rising semitones of the 'Desire' motif melt into the serene embrace of the final chord of B major, the effect can be like a revelation: for many listeners there is a moment of inner recognition, as though a voice from deep within has said, 'Of course!'

end of another piece of music: 'This is clearly an analogue of the satisfaction of the will which is enhanced through delay.' Wagner may have expanded the tonal language to a degree that no one before had thought possible, but in the end he reaffirms that language stupendously. It is surely significant that, in Wagner's operas wholly composed after the completion of *Tristan* (*Die Meistersinger*, *Götterdämmerung* and *Parsifal*), tonal language is strengthened still further: expanded, certainly, by the experience of writing *Tristan*, but not fundamentally undermined. Wagner is no more the prophetic forerunner of Schoenberg than Beethoven was to Wagner – however much Wagner might have tried to suggest otherwise in his Paris essay *Eine Pilgerfahrt zu Beethoven*.

Still, there is no denying the fact that Wagner's treatment of dissonance in *Tristan und Isolde* is revolutionary. But listeners who find talk of 'tonality' and 'harmonic resolutions' hard to follow need have no fear: part of *Tristan*'s extraordinary power is that its technical processes can be grasped on an intuitive or emotional level. Right at the start of the **Prelude** one can feel the pent-up longing in the 'Desire' motif. Its opening cello 'sigh', the pungent yet exquisite woodwind dissonance it lands on, and the oboe's achingly chromatic upward steps that follow, together feel like the very soul of unfulfilled longing – simultaneously intense pleasure and intense pain. The idea is heard again, rising then fragmenting, the silences in between each statement as powerfully suggestive as the idea itself; yet the search for fulfilment or relief is fruitless. This is the *Tristan* predicament in essence. Is desire unappeasable? Is renunciation and resignation the only answer (as Schopenhauer claimed) – or might sexual satisfaction itself lead to another kind of Nirvana, in which love finds its ultimate expression and satisfaction in death? Longer, more ardent themes (each in some way offshoots of the 'Desire' motif) build to an orgasmic climax, yet there is still no sense of release. The 'Desire' motif continues to sound, plaintively now, on woodwind; then another great sigh from cellos and basses peters out on a pizzicato G; this is the end of the Prelude, but in no sense is it a musical 'ending'.

What follows in the opera is masterly. The sailor's wistful song to his 'Irish maid' is heard unaccompanied. It begins on the note G (the note on which the Prelude ended), but although it has something of the character of a folksong, its chromatically tortuous first phrase subtly traces the outline of the 'Desire' motif – this ordinary sailor also has his painful longings. From this grows an operatic act which, though it is rich in change and musical drama, feels as seamless as a great symphonic movement. When, near the end of Act I, Tristan and Isolde drink from what they believe is the poisoned goblet, the 'Desire' motif is heard, almost exactly as it was at the beginning of the Prelude. Then as the lovers realize what has happened, they sing each other's names to the Prelude's ardent second motif. This extraordinary moment is at once the great dramatic turning-point of the first act, and a kind of symphonic 'recapitulation'. As the sailors' joyful cries are heard off-stage, more of the Prelude's motifs come cascading back in the orchestra. The rousing choral cheers and the lovers' increasingly frenzied vocal lines and orchestral accompaniment seem to belong to two different planes of existence. 'The King!' cries Kurvenal; 'What King?' Tristan replies. As Act I closes, the worlds of the 'Night of Love' and 'false deceiving day' stand revealed in opposition for the first time.

Why is day 'false' and 'deceiving'? Because it is in the daytime that we are most aware of duty, obligation, and what

> From this grows an operatic act which, though it is rich in change and musical drama, feels as seamless as a great symphonic movement.

we call 'rational' reality. All this is illusory, says Schopenhauer in *Die Welt als Wille und Vorstellung*: it is merely how our senses and perceptual apparatuses represent (*vorstellen*) the world to us. The reality behind it is the blind, craving will or desire (*Wille* has connotations of both), which we become more aware of at night: in dreams, imaginative fears, and quickened sexual desire. Act II of *Tristan und Isolde* is set entirely in the realm of night – at least until the shock arrival of King Marke and his retinue at the height of the lovers' ecstasy. Soon after the opening, throbbing string figures and a rising, velvet-toned bass clarinet figure create a sense of heightened anticipation: half delicious, half fearful. Then distant hunting-horn calls – musical cousins of the sailors' joyous cries at the end of Act I – signal the retreating power of day.

Later in Act II, as the lovers are reunited, the initial throbbing string figures and rising bass clarinet motif are allowed to build in rising sequences to a volcanic climax, more intense than anything in Act I. For a while their love duet sweeps all before it, but in time it quietens as their expression becomes more intimate. Now a syncopated rhythm spreads through the orchestra, creating a kind of 'fainting' effect. Wagner's freeing of rhythm from the straightforward muscular clarity of much Baroque and Classical music is another innovatory feature of *Tristan*, but one far less often commented on than its alleged undermining of tonality. The syncopated rhythms continue to pulse quietly as Brangäne sings her warning from the nearby tower, the orchestra now developing a languorous two-note motif associated moments before with the word 'Lie-be' ('Love'), and surrounding it with a fabulous weft of orchestral detail. Tristan and Isolde sing together again, their voices

> Tristan and Isolde sing together again, their voices weaving in and out of one of Wagner's most gorgeous and tender melodies. Night has united the lovers, and brought out the finest in Wagner the musical poet.

weaving in and out of one of Wagner's most gorgeous and tender melodies. Night has united the lovers, and brought out the finest in Wagner the musical poet. The violent interruption of Tristan and Isolde's love-dream by the return of King Marke and his hunting party only makes it seem the more desirable, and more poignant, in retrospect.

The contrast between this vision of erotic paradise, tragically cut short, and the opening of Act III is extreme. The four rising notes at the end of the 'Desire' motif are transformed into a sombre ascending figure for violins, starting right down on their lowest string, above a dark, two-chord cadence for the lower strings. The violins then continue to rise desolately, followed by a lamenting horn and solo cello figure that falls by chromatic steps as though unable to find a point of rest. The melancholic, endless rise and fall of the sea, the desolation of grey skies, and Tristan's emotional and physical pain are thus conveyed in the most vivid and haunting of sound symbols. After this the shepherd's sad, improvisatory piping (cor anglais), constantly circling around the same phrases, creates an effect close to timelessness, confirmed by the return of the opening sombre string cadences.

Here we encounter another of Wagner's innovations. Kurvenal's conversations with the delirious Tristan seem to strive away from this mood of eternal emptiness, ruin and decay, and yet each return of the shepherd's dolorous piping is a reminder that nothing has changed. This suspension of the sense of time passing, so essential in western symphonic music, and so integral to the compelling power of Act I, is like nothing before in opera. Tristan's ravings momentarily convince us that time is moving forward after all, then we hear that doleful cor anglais again and realize that it is all illusory, just as Schopenhauer said.

The turning-point of Act III is provided by Isolde's entry. Tristan's brief flicker of recognition is expressed as he sings her name to the ardent second theme from the Prelude (just as he did in Act I), only this time it dies on his lips. Only a moment earlier, as Isolde rushed in and sang her lover's name, the 'Desire' motif was heard. The tremendous effectiveness of this recapitulation is further proof of Wagner's mastery. Although echoes of these themes can be heard throughout the opera, Wagner is careful not to use them too often in their original forms; that way their return is all the more devastating, and the link to the similar recapitulation near the end of Act I acquires an extra dimension of tragic irony.

As with the *Ring*, more of these connections and cross-references reveal themselves on closer acquaintance, throwing new light or shade on words or actions which at first may seem of only passing significance. Discovering them is a journey that can fill a lifetime, and at each stage the meaning of individual moments – or perhaps even of the whole work – shifts subtly. Are Tristan and Isolde tragic figures: Romantic 'doomed lovers', though of an especially memorable and complex kind? Or are they 'victors', world-renouncers, as in the Schopenhauer-inspired Buddhist opera that Wagner began sketching in 1856? Can sexual fulfilment truly be a road to transcendence, or does death offer the only possibility of permanent release from the agony of desire? *Tristan und Isolde* provides no logical, consistent answer to any of these questions. Instead it objectifies them, holds them up for contemplation, in music of such power and beauty that, as Isolde yields herself to death's 'highest bliss' ('höchste Lust') in her Liebestod, we may feel that – for a moment at least – we too have found peace and resolution.

CD 2
track 1
www.naxosbooks.com

Die Meistersinger von Nürnberg
('The Mastersingers of Nuremberg')
(in Three Acts)

First Performance: June 21, 1868,
Royal Court and National Theatre, Munich

Synopsis

Website
www.naxosbooks.com

Act I Nuremberg in the mid-sixteenth century. Midsummer's Eve. The interior of St Katharine's Church. A service is just finishing. A young knight, Walther von Stolzing, has sold his estate and moved to Nuremberg, where he has fallen in love with Eva, daughter of the goldsmith Viet Pogner. Meeting Eva and her nurse Magdalene as the congregation leaves the church, he learns that her father has promised her in marriage to the winner of the song competition that is to take place on Midsummer's Day (we learn later that Eva is to have the casting vote). To enter, Walther must first join the guild of the mastersingers. Magdalene enlists the help of her admirer, the cobbler's apprentice David, to prepare Walther for entry into the guild. Pogner too is encouraging. The mastersingers assemble in the church. When Walther reveals that he learned the art of singing from a book, and from what he heard and felt in the forest, many of them are dismissive. Walther sings for them, while the town clerk, Sixtus Beckmesser, acts as 'marker' (adjudicator). Beckmesser is a pedant; moreover he wants Eva for himself. Not surprisingly he is sharply critical. The cobbler Hans Sachs senses something original and authentic in Walther's singing, but he is a lone voice, and Walther is declared to have failed the test. Walther leaves in disgust, while Sachs muses to himself.

Act II Evening. An alley between Pogner's and Sachs's houses. Magdalene tells Eva about Walther's failure at the test. Sachs cannot forget Walther's song as he tries to work on Beckmesser's shoes: 'Es klang so alt, und war doch so neu' ('It sounded so familiar, and yet so new'). Eva consults Sachs, whom she sees as a wise father figure. Cunningly he teases her about Walther, and when she flounces out angrily he realizes that she loves Walther and resolves to help her. Eva and Magdalene hatch a plot to foil Beckmesser, who has announced his intention to serenade Eva that evening. They will take each other's place: Beckmesser will be humiliated, and David might be provoked by jealousy into proposing to Magdalene. Eva and Walther decide to elope. The night-watchman's song is heard announcing ten o'clock. Beckmesser appears, carrying a lute, but Sachs continually interrupts him with an earthy cobbler's song about the biblical Eve ('Eva' in German). He agrees to listen to Beckmesser's song if he can act as marker, indicating any of Beckmesser's infringements of the guild rules by tapping the shoe he is working on. Stung by Sachs's increasingly frequent taps, Beckmesser tries to drown him out with his singing. This wakes some of the neighbors, among them David who – according to plan – thinks that Beckmesser is serenading Magdalene and wallops him with his cudgel. Soon the neighbors are all fighting, shrieking or hurling abuse; but the chaos comes to an end at the sound of the night-watchman's horn. Sachs drags David off Beckmesser and bundles Walther into his shop. When the watchman rounds the corner he is surprised to find that all is quiet again, as though nothing had happened.

Act III Midsummer morning. Sachs's workshop. David is

ashamed of his behavior the night before and begs forgiveness *The original* from Sachs. Feigning anger at first, Sachs is finally indulgent. *workshop of Hans* Left alone, Sachs reads from an old folio. Remembering how *Sachs, German* violence suddenly sprang up during the previous evening *poet and song-* he reflects on the stupidity and pointless violence of human *writer (1494–1576)* behavior: 'Wahn, Wahn! Überall Wahn!' ('Illusion, illusion! *on whom Wagner* Everywhere illusion'). Walther enters the room and reveals *based the character* that he has had a beautiful dream, in which a song came to *Hans Sachs in* Die him. Sachs agrees to listen, and helps him to understand how Meistersinger von he can submit to the mastersingers' rules without fettering Nürnberg his imagination: indeed his song will acquire surer and stronger wings. Innovation and tradition can and should be reconciled. Sachs and Walther leave together, then Beckmesser enters. Seeing the scrap of paper on which Sachs has noted down Walther's song, he thinks that Sachs himself is planning to enter the competition. Sachs returns and denies it all, but – to Beckmesser's astonishment – offers him the song, without telling him who the real author is. Eva enters, dressed splendidly for the song competition but downcast in expression. Then she sees Walther, in full knightly attire. The sight of her inspires him to compose a third verse for his song, which Sachs pronounces a true master-song. Turning aside he reveals, somewhat grudgingly, that his love for Eva has always been more than fatherly, but that he is determined to help her find true happiness. Eva pours out her gratitude to him, while he assures her that the sufferings of the legendary King Marke are not for him. Joined by Magdalene and David, the young couple and Sachs sing a rapturous quintet in honor of Walther's new song. The scene then changes to a meadow just outside the town. The song competition is ready to begin. Beckmesser goes first, but makes such a hash of the song given to him by Sachs that the onlookers burst out laughing. Enraged, he declares that Sachs is the true author. Sachs denies it, and calls Walther forward to demonstrate that the original, unbowdlerized version is a thing of genuine beauty. Walther's singing delights both the people and the mastersingers, and he is awarded the prize and Eva's hand. The guild offer Walther the gold chain of membership. At first Walther turns away haughtily; but Sachs takes him by the hand and urges him eloquently not to scorn tradition: 'Ehrt Eure deutschen Meister' ('Honor your German Masters'). Moved, Walther joins in the chorus of praise to 'Holy German Art' and Nuremberg's 'beloved Sachs'.

The Drama in Music

In 1828, just as he was beginning his studies with Christian Gottlieb Müller, the fifteen-year-old Wagner made a significant note in his pocketbook: 'Get to know Mozart'. The mature Wagner's admiration for Mozart was not unqualified, but that he learned from the earlier 'German Master' is evident on page after page of the score of *Die Meistersinger*.

Mozart is not usually the first name that comes to mind when listening to the solid, opulently harmonized march tune that opens the **Prelude**; but throughout the opera there are light, deft touches that suggest the influence of the composer of *Don Giovanni* (which Wagner first conducted in 1834). The humor is never heavy-handed, the wit neither overly ingenious nor stilted. Like Mozart in his comic operas, Wagner is able to imply laughter in his orchestral writing: a delicate trill or 'old-fashioned' ornament here, a scurrying descending scale there. Yet there is no suggestion that we are being ordered to laugh: Wagner's 'powerful drive of assertiveness' was never less in evidence than in the more intimate comic moments of *Die Meistersinger*.

CD 2
track 1

www.naxosbooks.com

Just as he was beginning his studies with Christian Gottlieb Müller, the fifteen-year-old Wagner made a significant note in his pocketbook: 'Get to know Mozart'.

There are two other features of the *Meistersinger* style that Mozart would have approved – at least in principle. More than in any of the other operas from the *Ring* onwards, the singers not only participate in the melodic phrases, they lead them. Walther's prizewinning song is the most obvious example, but there are countless others. The orchestra colors but does not dominate the melodic writing. As in *Siegfried*, and still more in *Götterdämmerung*, Wagner relaxes his earlier rule that there should only be one note per syllable; thus he allows the vocal lines to unfold more mellifluously. It is interesting to note that the one character who indulges in long, florid turns of musical phrase on single syllables is the ridiculous Beckmesser. Wagner's disgust at the overuse of such purely decorative devices is all too obvious. Mozart might also have smiled wryly to observe Wagner relaxing another of his Greek-inspired musico-dramatic rules: the law prohibiting ensemble writing – especially the kind of ensemble in which different characters sing different words simultaneously. Mozart's lively ensemble writing, with its quick-fire exchanges between voices and supple, characterful counterpoint, is one of the glories of his comic operas. Now, in *Die Meistersinger*, Wagner follows his example, to similarly glorious effect. In fact the great quintet in Act III is one of the high points of the opera, as touching, uplifting and sensuously beautifully as Walther's prizewinning song.

It is also possible that Wagner was deliberately following Mozart's example at two specific points in the drama: passages in which he indulges in something suspiciously like self-parody. In Act II of Mozart's *Don Giovanni*, the servant Leporello recoils when the on-stage band plays a tune from Mozart's own *Le nozze di Figaro* ('The Marriage of Figaro'). *Meistersinger*, as Sachs drowns out Beckmesser's serenade in Act II with his own coarse cobbler's song, Wagner alludes to Siegfried's none-too-subtle forging song in the *Ring*. Then there are the gentle orchestral references to *Tristan und Isolde* in Act III as Sachs announces that he has no intention of playing King Marke – perhaps an admission on Wagner's part that Marke's nobility of spirit might after all be too good to be true.

Die Meistersinger is one of Wagner's longer operas. And yet it seems almost continually on the move: the music always fluid, changeable, mercurial.

Equally Mozartian is the remarkable pace of Wagner's comedy. *Die Meistersinger* is one of Wagner's longer operas. And yet it seems almost continually on the move: the music always fluid, changeable, mercurial. The timeless desolation of *Tristan*'s Act III feels impossibly remote. The final act of *Meistersinger* is one of Wagner's biggest single structures (in most performances it easily fills two hours); but, so long as the conducting is not ponderously reverential, the time hurtles by. Rossini's famous jibe that Wagner's music 'has lovely moments but awful quarters of an hour' could not be less appropriate than here.

Another 'German Master' whose influence can be felt in the music of *Die Meistersinger* is Johann Sebastian Bach. Bach had been Kapellmeister in Wagner's home town of Leipzig, but as a young man Wagner had attached little importance to this. Like many musicians of the early nineteenth century, he appears to have regarded Bach's music as dry and archaic, useful only for didactic purposes. His view had begun to change, however, by the time he became Kapellmeister at the Dresden court. It was there that he conducted Bach's motet *Singet dem Herrn* – a bold and unusual choice for the time. The most obviously Bachian passage in *Meistersinger* is the beginning of Act I, where the phrases of a Lutheran hymn tune, sung by the choir, are punctuated by short instrumental passages, with the occasional touch of free imitation between the instruments. Similar treatment of Lutheran hymns can be found in many of Bach's church cantatas, and in the two great Passions. But Wagner does not simply imitate obvious Bachian practices. It is clear that he had by this time learned much from the example of Bach's contrapuntal writing – the kind of musical texture in which a number of vocal or instrumental lines follow their own independent courses, each line taking its turn to be 'first among equals'. From this point of view the closing section of the Prelude is a *tour de force*; all the main motifs and melodic lines weave in and out of each other, creating an orchestral texture of extraordinary richness, alive on many levels at once. The spirit of Bach is present in the contrapuntal writing, but without a hint of Baroque pastiche.

There is one other German Master – not a composer (or rather not purely a composer) this time – who is saluted in *Die Meistersinger*: the sixteenth-century great religious reformer Martin Luther. The scene of German *bürgerlich* ('bourgeois') peace, prosperity and cultural flowering painted by Wagner in

Die Meistersinger gives no hint of the bloody upheavals that had followed in the wake of the Lutheran Reformation. The invocation of Luther through the hymn would have had other resonances for patriotic Germans in the years leading up to, and after, the establishment of the German Second Reich. Luther's translation of the Bible is generally seen as a defining moment in the story of the emergence of the modern German language. It was a symbol of German cultural unity for many at a time when the German peoples were still divided into states, kingdoms and duchies, and also a reminder that modern Europe's liberation from subjugation to papal authority had begun in Germany. Luther had also been responsible for creating a new form of musical worship: the vernacular hymn or 'chorale', through which ordinary members of the congregation could address God in their own tongue in simple, often folk-derived tunes. That a Lutheran-style chorale should be the first thing heard as the curtain goes up on *Die Meistersinger* is enormously significant.

> The lightness of touch characteristic of so much of *Die Meistersinger* is a welcome revelation for those whose experience of Wagner encompasses extracts from the *Ring* or *Tristan und Isolde*. Equally refreshing is the discovery of how tender and affectionate Wagner's comedy can be.

This chorale was written by Wagner himself, and the fact that non-German listeners have sometimes taken it for a traditional tune shows how thoroughly Wagner's study of German hymns and folk tunes paid off. If listeners know only the Prelude to *Meistersinger* it can be a wonderful surprise to discover how, in the opera, the Prelude's 'ending' flows straight into the first phrase of the chorale. Again Wagner shows himself to be master of what he called 'the art of transition'.

The lightness of touch characteristic of so much of *Die Meistersinger* is a welcome revelation for those whose experience of Wagner encompasses extracts from the *Ring* or *Tristan und Isolde*. Equally refreshing is the discovery of how tender and affectionate Wagner's comedy can be. The composer Sir John Tavener speaks for many when he says that, for him, the truly transcendent element in Mozart's comic operas is that 'he forgives all his characters'. This might also be said of Wagner. True, it is questionable whether he ultimately forgives Beckmesser. The final stage direction for Beckmesser describes him as disappearing into the crowd after his humiliation at the competition; yet presumably he is still there, somewhere, possibly even joining in the hymn to Sachs at the end. And in spite of Sachs's sombre diagnosis of the human condition in Act III (the wonderful 'Wahn, Wahn! Überall Wahn!' monologue), he is fundamentally inclined to look kindly on human folly, Beckmesser's apparently included.

Some have pointed to Sachs's Act III monologue as proof that the message of *Die Meistersinger* is essentially Schopenhauerian: Sachs's recognition of the prevalence of illusion in human affairs is followed by his readiness to give up Eva to the man she really loves. The dignified yet sorrowful orchestral prelude to Act III, described by Wagner as a musical portrait of Sachs, seems to endorse such an interpretation. Then there are the cobbler's words when Walther reveals that his new song has come to him in a dream:

> *My friend, it is precisely the poet's work to interpret and give form to his dreamings. Believe me, man's truest illusion is revealed to him in dreams; the whole of poetry and verse is nothing but the true interpretation of dreams.*

When it came to the importance of dreams, Wagner was in complete agreement with Schopenhauer.

Yet the interpretation of *Die Meistersinger* as a

Schopenhauerian comedy seems far-fetched. It is, after all, a comedy with a more-or-less traditional happy ending: lovers joyously united, honest burghers uniting in praise of their culture and its embodiment in the wise cobbler–poet Sachs. Human beings may succumb to illusion from time to time, but in general human nature is observed with genial good humor, even love. The 'expanded' tonal harmony developed in *Tristan und Isolde* is present here too, but in *Meistersinger* it is mostly used not to convey the pain of desire (which led Schopenhauer to such melancholy conclusions) but to lend a warm, ripe glow to the otherwise solidly tonal language. Dissonance is quickly resolved; or, when a harmony remains suspended (as when Sachs enjoys the scent of the lilac near the beginning of in Act II), it conveys a kind of mysterious delight rather than unappeasable longing. Perhaps the scent itself comes from that nocturnal world of dreams where Walther will find his prizewinning song. Part of the magic of *Die Meistersinger* is the sense it communicates of being poised between solid but very likeable (and far from illusory) reality and the realm of the imagination, from which music and poetry can come to us like the scent of lilac, drifting in the air on a midsummer's eve. If in the process Wagner reveals himself as something of an 'armchair Schopenhauerian' – content to derive inspiration and ideas from the great philosopher while drawing back from the austerity of world-renunciation – then so much the better for operatic comedy.

Parsifal

Bühnenweihfestspiel ('Stage Consecration Drama')
in Three Acts

First Performance: July 26, 1882,
Festival Theatre (Festspielhaus), Bayreuth

Synopsis

Act I A forest near the castle of the Holy Grail. The elderly but still vigorous Gurnemanz rouses two young squires who are sleeping beneath a tree. They talk of their sick King, Amfortas, and of his mysterious wound that will not heal. Gurnemanz knows that only one thing can save Amfortas: the arrival of a pure fool made wise by compassion ('Durch Mitleid wissend, der reine Tor'). Kundry arrives in almost frenzied excitement. She has brought a balsam from Arabia that might assuage the King's pain. The King is carried in. His suffering has eased, but he too knows that the prophecy of the redeeming fool is his only hope. The Grail knights react in horror when a swan flutters in, mortally wounded by an arrow. The killer is a strange youth, possibly of noble birth, but who appears to know nothing about himself, his parents, nor even his own name. Kundry, however, tells him that she saw his mother die. The youth reacts in fury. Gurnemanz restrains him, and then begins to wonder if this strange youth might be the prophesied redeemer. Gurnemanz leads him to the castle of the Grail. At the shrine, he and the youth watch the ritual of the unveiling of the Grail. The sick Amfortas refuses to perform the ceremony, but under pressure from his father Titurel he gives in. Gurnemanz watches the youth, who is clearly moved, but totally uncomprehending. Finally Gurnemanz dismisses him: he is just a fool after all.

Act II Klingsor's magic castle. The magician Klingsor is the implacable enemy of the Grail and its guardians. Moreover Kundry is in his power. He wakes her, and orders her to ensnare the innocent youth who is on his way to the castle. Klingsor has the spear that pierced Christ on the cross, and that caused Amfortas's wound. He will now use it against the youth. In the gardens Klingsor's flower maidens try to seduce the youth, but he rejects them. Suddenly he hears Kundry calling 'Parsifal', and knows at once that it is his own name. Kundry plays on Parsifal's feelings of guilt about his mother's death, at the same time subtly working her charm upon him. She kisses him on the lips, but the awakening of sexual desire in Parsifal brings with it his first understanding of human suffering. 'Amfortas!' he cries: 'Die Wunde!' ('The wound!'). Enraged by Parsifal's sudden withdrawal from her, Kundry summons Klingsor, who hurls the spear at Parsifal; but Parsifal seizes it and makes the sign of the Cross, at which the castle collapses as the gardens wither to nothing. 'You know where you can find me again', Parsifal tells Kundry, and leaves.

Act III An orchestral prelude depicts Parsifal's long and desperate search for the Grail castle – according to legend those who seek it can never find it, except at the Grail's own behest. The curtain rises on the landscape surrounding the Grail castle. Now older and frailer, Gurnemanz has become a hermit. Titurel is dead, and Amfortas refuses to perform the unveiling of the Grail. Gurnemanz finds Kundry prostrate, dressed as a penitent: she tells him that she now wants only to serve ('Dienen, dienen'). A strange knight enters clad in black armor, carrying a spear. Astonished, Gurnemanz recognizes him as the fool he drove away, long ago, and realizes that the time of salvation has come at last. Gurnemanz cleanses Parsifal in the holy spring and anoints him the new King of the Grail. Looking around him, Parsifal understands that Good Friday has come, and that nature has regained its innocence. Parsifal kisses Kundry's head. She who once mocked Christ on the Cross, and was condemned to wander eternally for her sin, is now forgiven. The scene changes to the Grail castle. The knights urge Amfortas to unveil the Grail, but, delirious with pain and despair, he orders them to kill him. But it is Parsifal who steps forward: the weapon that wounded Amfortas will now heal him. The spear itself is now cleansed of evil and is holy again. Parsifal takes the Grail from the shrine and kneels in prayer. As the chorus sing of how redemption has come to the redeemer ('Erlösung dem Erlöser') a dove descends over Parsifal's head, and Kundry falls lifeless, finally at peace.

The Drama in Music

CD 2
track 5

www.naxosbooks.com

Claude Debussy described the orchestral writing in *Parsifal* as 'lit up from within'. It is a wonderful description, and anyone who knows the opera's **Prelude** – often performed independently in concert – will readily agree. A particularly beautiful illustration of this technique of 'inner illumination' can be found very near the start of the Prelude. Quietly and with great delicacy the string players move their bows rapidly backwards and forwards across the strings, while in the background flutes and clarinets play simple chords of A flat major in a gentle throbbing rhythm. The strings create a misty, tremulous sound, through which the woodwind chords sound like pulsations of light. This follows a passage which – in a very different way from Act III of *Tristan und Isolde* – manages to convey a sense of defying the passage of time. At the very beginning, muted strings and woodwind present a long, aspiring theme, with something of the rhythmic freedom that Wagner discovered in *Tristan*. Although the conductor maintains a steady, slow tempo, the theme seems to float free of the beat – an effect rather like the measureless unfolding of traditional Roman Catholic plainchant.

A little later in the Prelude, brass play a noble extended cadence, whose final rising phrase is echoed by the high woodwind – more 'light upon light'. This figure is in fact a quotation: the so-called 'Dresden Amen', which has been used in the Lutheran Church since the eighteenth century; it was also quoted by Mendelssohn in his 'Reformation' Symphony as a symbol of enduring faith. After this comes a majestic brass theme, rising in sequence into the key of D major, harmonically as far as possible from the home key of A flat. Wagner told Cosima that this modulation from A flat to D represented for him 'the spreading of the tender revelation throughout the whole world' (a statement apparently ignored by those who have tried to interpret *Parsifal* as an exclusively Aryan fantasy). After this the strings play the Dresden Amen, quietly but this time without mutes, the sound thus much brighter than at the beginning – another effect of illumination. There is darkness too in the Prelude, but it is a darkness which, to borrow a phrase from T.S. Eliot, 'declares the glory of light'. The orchestra develops the tortuously chromatic motifs associated with the spear and Amfortas's suffering, through clouds of string tremolos; but at the end of the Prelude the woodwind's high pulsating chords are heard again, as the violins rise up to a stratospheric high E flat. Light prevails.

Even listeners who are normally resistant to religious imagery can find the Prelude to *Parsifal* – and indeed the whole opera – inexplicably moving. Debussy, for one, was no believer, and made strenuous efforts to distance himself from what he saw as *Parsifal*'s ethical and religious message; and yet for him the score remained 'one of the most beautiful monuments ever raised to music.' Still more strikingly, Wagner's renegade former disciple Nietzsche, who had poured scorn on *Parsifal* in *Der Fall Wagner*, confided to his sister, 'I cannot think of [the Prelude] without feeling violently shaken, so elevated was I by it, so deeply moved.' Some have responded to this paradox by trying to read something sinister within the opera's otherworldly beauty. They point

> Even listeners who are normally resistant to religious imagery can find the Prelude to *Parsifal* – and indeed the whole opera – inexplicably moving.

to Wagner's racial theorising – which was increasingly bizarre at the time of writing *Parsifal* – and ingeniously reinterpret the story as a dark racist allegory. And yet, if this alleged 'racist' message (redemption through 'the blood' in a cultural sense?) was so important to Wagner, why did he not take the trouble to make it more explicit? Though there were some who found Wagner's ideas obnoxious at the time, in late-nineteenth-century Europe there was not the widespread rejection of racial theories that prevails (at least in public) today. In any case, as the Wagner expert John Deathridge puts it, trenchantly:

> *whether* Parsifal *is a sinister milleniarist fantasy about the redemption of an Aryan Jesus from Judaism... or just a feeble Armageddon cocktail with large twists of Schopenhauer, critics of its supposed inhumanity will always find it hard to account for the fascinating beauty of its score and the inconvenient fact that militancy and aggression could not be further removed from its central idea.*

Another 'inconvenient fact' is that Adolf Hitler was one person who felt decidedly uncomfortable with *Parsifal*. Whether it was the opera's religious content, its elevation of wisdom achieved through compassion, or what some have seen as its latent homoerotic element that Hitler balked at is hard to say. But if Wagner had intended some kind of racial allegory in *Parsifal*, the Nazis would have had none of it.

So what is *Parsifal's* 'central idea'? That surely is clear enough in the libretto, and still more in Wagner's musical treatment of it. Parsifal's innocence at the beginning of the opera is not an attractive quality; it is more like blank stupidity. His discovery of compassion at the climax of Act II is the redeeming, transfiguring moment; but this compassion is not the kind of pity that raises itself above the object it claims to feel sorry for. The crucial German word *Mitleid* preserves exactly the sense of the Latin *compassio* – 'suffer with' someone or something. It is Parsifal's discovery of the pain of sexual longing (awakened by Kundry's kiss) that brings him the sudden realization of what Amfortas's suffering must be like. As Schopenhauer said, the experience of intense desire can itself be like the agony of an open wound. Wagner's music registers this with far more eloquence than the words alone could possibly convey. As Kundry kisses him, a figure that sounds increasingly like the rising four-note chromatic pendant to the *Tristan* 'Desire' motif is heard in the orchestra, merging in greater agitation into the motifs associated with the spear and Amfortas's suffering. Parsifal cries 'Amfortas!' to the accompaniment of an astonishing discord – which looks ahead to the anguished harmony one might find in late Mahler. As Parsifal remembers the wound, this chord ripples up and down in the strings, transforming itself into a downward-plunging figure of extraordinary desolate power. It is this figure, and its attendant wild dissonance, that forms the climax of the harmonically tortuous orchestral prelude to Act III. Its significance there is

> As Schopenhauer said, the experience of intense desire can itself be like the agony of an open wound. Wagner's music registers this with far more eloquence than the words alone could possibly convey.

clear: while Parsifal searches desperately for the castle of the Grail, Amfortas's suffering goes on, as far from resolution as ever.

The notion of wisdom achieved through compassion is allotted a distinctive musical motif of its own, associated with the words 'Durch Mitleid wissend, der reine Tor'. This motif is not heard in the opera's Prelude, which makes good dramatic sense, as in Act I it only slowly begins to dawn on Gurnemanz that Parsifal could be the prophesied fool. At first it is just hinted at in the orchestra, as a background to Gurnemanz's words 'Toren wir, auf Lindrung da zu hoffen' ('We are fools to hope for help in that'), as one of the knights tells how herbs have failed to assuage Amfortas's torment. Gurnemanz only spells it out later in Act I, just before the wounded swan flutters onto the stage and Parsifal makes his first appearance. But Wagner is careful to avoid associating it directly with Parsifal at this point; indeed the shock of the swan's killing temporarily takes the memory of that motif away from the forefront of the listener's mind. When, at the end of Act I, the phrase 'Durch Mitleid wissend, der reine Tor' is sung out by an alto soloist, from high in the dome of the shrine, the effect of remoteness is emotional as well as physical: much will have to happen before the prophecy becomes reality. That happens in the music only at the end of the opera. Just after Parsifal has healed Amfortas's wound with the spear, the 'Wisdom through Compassion' motif rises and extends sequentially as Parsifal explains all: 'Gesegnet sei dein Leiden, das Mitleid's höchste Kraft, und reinsten Wissens Macht dem zagen Toren gab!' ('Blessed be your suffering, that brought compassion's highest power and the pure might of wisdom to the timorous fool'). So much for the notion that Parsifal's talk of *Kraft* ('power') and *Macht* ('might') have anything to do with German militarism.

There are, admittedly, uncomfortable elements for many in *Parsifal*. Seeing Kundry wretched and abased in Act III in the theatre for the first time can be acutely disturbing, and it smacks of unacknowledged sadomasochism on Wagner's part. This moment may reveal a fundamental strain of misogyny in his character; but it should be remembered that for Wagner Kundry was yet another incarnation of the 'Wandering Jew' figure that had so fascinated him – and elicited his compassion – in *Der Fliegende Holländer*. In *Parsifal* his music now elicits our compassion for Kundry far more movingly. It is also relevant to ask how the creator of the splendid Brünnhilde in the *Ring* could possibly have been an uncomplicated misogynist. Less morally controversial, though still difficult for some listeners to take, are the possible homoerotic elements. Apart from Kundry and those fleetingly glimpsed flower maidens (all morally dubious figures), *Parsifal* is a very homocentric opera. Is there any sexual significance in the fact that Wagner's last, and most ecstatically glorified, redeemer figure is a beautiful young man and not a woman? And then there is Parsifal's spear and Amfortas's wound: one doesn't have to be a Freudian to scent erotic possibilities here – especially when Wagner's music seems to be pointing us in that direction anyway.

That there are no adequate straightforward answers to any of these questions is part of the fascination of *Parsifal*. Yet there are also times when the music seems to speak with astonishing directness to something deep within us, however much our rational selves may flounder about in fruitless efforts to explain what we feel. These are those moments that Thomas Mann described as 'sudden glimpses into things of profound and moving significance'.

As Mann himself half sensed, there is more to this than 'wizardry' and 'cunning'. No better example of this exists than the ending of *Parsifal*. As Parsifal kneels before the Grail, the opera's leading motifs interweave and encircle one another as the music returns to the Prelude's serene, luminous A flat major. The counterpointing of these ideas is wonderfully elegant, the orchestration gorgeous; but that hardly begins to explain the total effect. The coming-together of the motifs, so that they sound like offshoots of the same musical essence, feels very like a symbol of integration on a spiritual level: it is compassion, Wagner seems to say, that can heal the wounds and divisions in the human soul.

If in the end he was only able to express that vision in his art – if in his life and prose works he continued to ignore the messages in his dreams about his paranoid obsessions – it is a matter for painful regret. Yet one can feel profoundly grateful that Wagner was able to express his vision at all.

Personalities

Apel, Theodor (1811–1867): Friend of Wagner at Leipzig University, where he initially studied law but turned to poetry and drama. Joined the young Wagner on summer holiday in Bohemia in 1834. Apel helped Wagner financially on a number of occasions.

Bakunin, Mikhail (1814–1876): Leading Russian anarchist and advocate of violent struggle. Wagner met Bakunin frequently in Dresden, and assisted him in some of his revolutionary activities in the uprising of 1849.

Berlioz, Hector (1803–1869): French composer. A pioneer in Romantic music, he was widely misunderstood and underestimated in his own lifetime. Wagner learned a great deal from Berlioz, but ultimately felt too distant from the Frenchman's aims and ideals to form a lasting friendship.

Bismarck, Prince Otto Eduard Leopold von (1815–1898): Prussian statesman. Appointed prime minister of Prussia in 1862 and first chancellor of the new German Reich in 1871. Initially repelled by his policies, Wagner eventually hailed him as the architect of German unity, trying unsuccessfully to win his support for the Bayreuth Festival.

Bülow, Hans (Guido) von (1830–1894): German conductor and pianist, and devotee of Wagner. Even after his first wife Cosima left him and took up with Wagner, resulting in divorce in 1870, he continued to champion the composer's music.

Cornelius, (Carl August) Peter (1824–1874): German composer. Met Wagner in Vienna in the early 1860s and was drawn (despite reservations) into the composer's intimate circle.

Dorn, Heinrich Ludwig Egmont (1804–1892). German composer and conductor. Gave first performance of the young Wagner's notorious 'Drum-beat Overture' in Leipzig. Dorn later succeeded Wagner as music director at the Riga theatre.

Feuerbach, Ludwig Andreas (1804–1872): German philosopher. Feuerbach argued a humanist philosophy which nevertheless recognized important truths in Christianity, especially the elevation of love above the moral law. He was an important discovery of Wagner's in the composer's Paris years, and Feuerbach's idea of love continued to influence him even after he was introduced to the views of the more pessimistic Schopenhauer.

Geyer, Ludwig (1779–1821): German actor and painter. Friend of the Wagner family and Wagner's stepfather from 1814. After Wagner's death a rumor grew that Geyer was the composer's real father.

Gobineau, Count Joseph-Arthur de (1816–1882): French diplomat, author, historian and racial theorist. Visited Wagner at Bayreuth in 1881–2. Wagner partly shared Gobineau's beliefs about the inequality of human races, though he was inclined to be less pessimistic about the possibility of cultural 'redemption'.

Hanslick, Eduard (1825–1904): Prague-born Austrian writer on music and aesthetics. Hugely influential as a critic, Hanslick was a powerful opponent of Wagner's music and ideas. The figure of Beckmesser in *Die Meistersinger* was partly conceived as a caricature of Hanslick.

Heine, Heinrich (1797–1856): German poet and important inspiration for the Young Germany movement. Wagner met Heine during his Paris years, having already drawn on his writings for *Der fliegende Holländer*. Heine may also have influenced Wagner's conception of the mythical world of the *Ring*.

Herwegh, Georg (1817–1875): German poet and political activist. Lived in exile from 1839 in Switzerland, where he continued to support revolutionary activities and help refugees. It was Herwegh who introduced Wagner to the philosophy of Schopenhauer.

Joukovsky, Paul von (1845–1912): Russian painter. Became member of Wagner's intimate circle during the latter's stay in Naples in 1880. Designed sets and costumes for *Parsifal*.

Laube, Heinrich (1806–1884): German writer and critic and a leading member of Young Germany. His radical politics, sustained in the face of official persecution, made a strong impression on the young Wagner.

Laussot, Jessie, *née* **Taylor (?1829–1905):** English-born wife of a Bordeaux wine merchant, and passionate supporter of Wagner. She offered him financial support, and also had a brief affair with him.

Lehrs, Samuel (1806–1843): German philologist and close friend of Wagner during the composer's Paris years. Lehrs introduced Wagner to many new intellectual developments and gave him important information on the Tannhäuser and Lohengrin legends.

Levi, Hermann (1839–1900): German conductor. He became a passionate advocate of Wagner, and conducted the first performance of *Parsifal* in 1882. Wagner welcomed Levi's support, despite the latter's Jewishness.

Liszt, Franz (1811–1886): Hungarian composer and virtuoso pianist. Liszt met Wagner in Paris in 1841, but their friendship grew when Liszt began to promote Wagner's music. Wagner admired Liszt's musical innovations, and as composers they learned a great deal from each other.

Ludwig II, King of Bavaria (1845–1886): Crowned in 1864 at the age of eighteen, Ludwig adored Wagner's music, and gave the composer invaluable material and emotional support. Wagner's affair with Cosima von Bülow placed a great strain on their relationship, but Ludwig remained devoted to the music, and gave timely support to the Bayreuth project. Eccentric and unstable, he was declared insane and was deposed in 1886; soon afterwards he was discovered drowned in Lake Starnberg in mysterious circumstances.

Marschner, Heinrich (August) (1795–1861): German composer. Music director, Dresden (1824–6) and Kapellmeister at Leipzig (1827–30). Though rarely performed today, his music was a key influence on the development of German Romantic opera, and made a great impression on the young Wagner.

Mendelssohn (-Bartholdy), Felix (1809–1847): German composer, pianist; also conductor, significantly at the Leipzig Gewandhaus from 1835 to 1847. Although Wagner condemned both his conducting style and compositions (that Mendelssohn was Jewish was unquestionably influential), he was influenced by the older man's music.

Meyerbeer, Giacomo [b. Jakob Liebemann Beer] (1791–1864): German-born composer and child-prodigy pianist. Made his home in Paris, where he dominated the operatic scene. Meyerbeer made some efforts to help Wagner during the latter's Paris years and afterwards, but Wagner remained bitterly suspicious of him, the resentment fuelling his anti-Semitic prejudices.

Müller, Christian Gottlieb (1800–1863): German instrumentalist and conductor. Wagner studied harmony with him in Leipzig from 1828 to 1831.

Nietzsche, Friedrich (1844–1900): German philosopher, appointed professor of classical philology at Basle University at the age of twenty-four. Initially enthralled by Wagner, he became a member of the composer's intimate circle in the early 1870s, but later turned against both the man and his music, branding him as a symptom of German cultural decadence. Even so, Nietzsche's idea of the 'Superman' was almost certainly influenced by the experience of knowing Wagner. Nietzsche died insane, possibly as a result of tertiary syphilis.

Richter, Hans (1843–1916): Hungarian-born Austrian conductor. Assistant to Wagner at Tribschen, he later conducted the first complete performance of the *Ring* cycle, not entirely to Wagner's satisfaction. He became a leading figure in British musical life as conductor of the Hallé Orchestra and the London Symphony Orchestra.

Ritter, Julie, *née* **Momma (1794–1869):** Friend and supporter of Wagner from his period as Kapellmeister in Dresden onwards. Together with Jessie Laussot she organized an annual income for Wagner, and continued to help him after the scandal of his affair with Jessie.

Ritter, Karl (1830–1891): Son of Julie Ritter. Worked with Wagner during his exile in Zurich, and went with him to Venice after the crisis of Wagner's affair with Mathilde Wesendonck.

Röckel, August (1814–1876): German composer and conductor. Fellow Kapellmeister of Wagner at Dresden, he shared in the latter's revolutionary activities, for which he spent thirteen years in prison.

Schnorr von Carolsfeld, Ludwig (1836–1865): German tenor. Outstanding as Tannhäuser and Lohengrin, he created the role of Tristan in 1865. His death only three weeks after the premiere of *Tristan* helped to foster the legend that the opera was unperformable.

Schnorr von Carolsfeld, Malvina, *née* **Garrigues (1825– 1904):** Copenhagen-born soprano, wife of Ludwig Schnorr von Carolsfeld, and creator of the role of Isolde. Possibly inspired by jealousy, she revealed the truth about Wagner's affair with Cosima to Ludwig II.

Schopenhauer, Arthur (1788–1860): German philosopher. Neglected for most of his life, he was suddenly catapulted to fame in 1853. Shortly afterwards, Wagner read and was enormously impressed by Schopenhauer's *magnum opus Die Welt als Wille and Vorstellung* ('The World as Will and Representation'), especially by Schopenhauer's pessimistic world-view, and his teachings about world-renunciation and compassion. Schopenhauer's elevation of music as supreme among the arts also affected the development of Wagner's ideas about music drama. Wagner sent him a copy of the *Ring* poem, but the two men never met.

Schröder-Devrient, Wilhelmine (1804–1860): German soprano, famed especially for the dramatic power of her interpretations. Her performance in the role of Leonore in Beethoven's *Fidelio* in Dresden in 1829 left a lasting impression on Wagner. Later she created the role of Adriano in Wagner's *Rienzi.*

Schumann, Robert (1810–1856): German composer, pianist and critic. Schumann initially encouraged Wagner, but he was later more attracted to neo-classical ideals which he found personified in the young Brahms. He died insane.

Wagner, Albert (1799–1874): Elder brother of the composer. Tenor and actor at various German theatres, he eventually became director at the Berlin Court Theatre.

Wagner, Cosima (1837–1930): Daughter of the Countess Marie d'Agoult by Franz Liszt. She married the conductor Hans von Bülow in 1857, but began an affair with Wagner six years later, bearing him three children out of wedlock. They married in 1870. Devoted to her second husband and his cause, Cosima remained director of the Bayreuth Festival for twenty-three years after Wagner's death.

Wagner, Christine Wilhelmine ('Minna'), *née* **Planer (1809–1866):** German actress and the composer's first wife. Although Minna was loyal to Wagner for many years, often in great hardship, his revolutionary activities, exile, and affair with Mathilde Wesendonck forced them further and further apart.

Wagner, Rosalie [later Rosalie Marbach] (1803–1837): Elder sister of Wagner. Actress, with notable successes in Prague and Leipzig. Despite her disapproval of his youthful excesses, Rosalie remained Wagner's favorite sister, and her sudden death, only a year after her marriage, was a serious blow.

Wagner, Siegfried (Helferich Richard) (1869–1930): German composer and conductor, son of Richard Wagner. On his mother's retirement in 1906, Siegfried assumed directorship of the Bayreuth Festival, and was somewhat less hostile to innovations than she had been. Siegfried's birth, a source of great joy to Wagner, was celebrated in the composer's *Siegfried Idyll.*

Weinlig, Christian Theodor (1780–1842): German organist and composer. Wagner studied composition with Weinlig in 1831, at which time the latter was Kantor at the Leipzig Thomaskirche.

Wesendonck, Mathilde, *née* **Luckemeyer (1828–1902):** German poet and wife of Wagner's patron Otto Wesendonck. Her passionate relationship with Wagner, and the guilt and suffering it caused, left powerful imprints on the opera *Tristan und Isolde*. Wagner set five of Mathilde's poems for his *Wesendonck Lieder*.

Wesendonck, Otto (1815–1896): German businessman. Having made his fortune as a silk importer, Otto retired to Zurich where he found a new *raison d'être* as Wagner's patron. He continued to support Wagner even after discovering the composer's affair with his wife Mathilde, which forced Wagner to leave Zurich.

Selected Bibliography

Adorno, Theodor, trans. Rodney Livingstone, *In Search of Wagner*, London, 1981

Beckett, Lucy, *Richard Wagner: 'Parsifal'*, Cambridge, 1981

Bekker, Paul, Eng. trans., *Richard Wagner: His Life in his Work*, London, 1931

Burbidge, Peter and **Sutton**, Richard, eds, *The Wagner Companion*, London, 1979

Burrell, Mary, *Richard Wagner: His Life and Works from 1813 to 1834*, London, 1898

Cooke, Deryck, *I Saw the World End: A Study of Wagner's 'Ring'*, London, 1979

Dalhaus, Carl, trans. Mary Whittall, *Richard Wagner's Music Dramas*, Cambridge, 1979

DiGaetani, John Louis, ed., *Penetrating Wagner's Ring: An Anthology*, Cranbury, New Jersey and London, 1978

Donington, Robert: *Wagner's 'Ring' and its Symbols: The Music and the Myth*, London, 1963

Ellis, William Ashton, *Life of Richard Wagner* (6 vols), London, 1900–08

Fischer-Dieskau, Dietrich, Eng. trans., *Wagner and Nietzsche*, New York, 1976, London, 1978

Gregor-Dellin, Martin, Eng. trans., abridged, *Richard Wagner: His Life, His Work, His Century*, London, 1983

Gutman, Robert, *Richard Wagner: The Man, His Mind, and His Music*, London, 1968

Hollinrake, Roger, *Nietzsche, Wagner, and the Philosophy of Pessimism*, London, 1982

Holloway, Robin, *Debussy and Wagner*, London, 1979

Magee, Bryan, *Aspects of Wagner*, London, 1968

Magee, Bryan, *Wagner and Philosophy*, London, 2000

Millington, Barry, *Wagner*, London, 1984; rev. edition, Princeton, 1992

Millington, Barry, ed., *The Wagner Compendium*, London, 1992

Müller, U. and **Wapnewski**, P., eds, *Wagner Handbook*, Cambridge (MA) and London, 1992

Newman, Ernest, *The Life of Richard Wagner* (4 vols), London, 1933–47

Newman, Ernest, *Wagner as Man and Artist*, London, 1924

Newman, Ernest, *Wagner Nights*, London, 1949

Sabor, Rudolph, *The Real Wagner*, London, 1987

Shaw, George Bernard, *The Perfect Wagnerite: A Commentary on the Niblung's Ring*, London, 1898

Skelton, Geoffrey, *Richard and Cosima Wagner: A Biography of a Marriage*, London, 1982

Skelton, Geoffrey, *Wagner in Thought and Practice*, London, 1991

Spotts, Frederic, *Bayreuth: A History of the Wagner Festival*, New Haven and London, 1994

Stein, Jack M., *Richard Wagner and the Synthesis of the Arts*, Detroit, 1960

Taylor, Ronald, *Richard Wagner: His Life, Art and Thought*, London, 1979

Wagner, Cosima, trans. Geoffrey Skelton, *Diaries* (2 vols), London, 1978 and 1980

Wagner, Richard, ed. & trans. Stewart Spencer and Barry Millington, *Selected Letters of Richard Wagner*, London, 1987

Warrack, John, *Richard Wagner: 'Die Meistersinger von Nürnberg'*, Cambridge, 1994

Watson, Derek, *Richard Wagner: A Biography*, London, 1979

Weiner, Marc A., *Richard Wagner and the Anti-Semitic Imagination*, Lincoln (NE) and London, 1995

Westernhagen, Curt von, trans. Mary Whittall, *Wagner: A Biography* (2 vols), Cambridge, 1978

Wolzogen, Hans von, Eng. trans., *Guide through the Music of R. Wagner's 'The Ring of the Nibelung'*, London, 1882

Glossary

Allegro (It.) 'Lively', 'quick'. A tempo marking indicating a vigorous style or speed. It can also refer to a complete movement of a symphony, concerto or sonata, or to a section of a movement in a lively tempo.

Aria (It.) 'Air'. Since the eighteenth century, a substantial, usually self-contained piece for solo voice with instrumental or orchestral accompaniment. In operas, arias form integral parts of the drama while remaining performable as separate items.

Ballet In opera, extensive danced sections, often spectacularly staged, were highly popular in the nineteenth century, especially in Paris. They were usually placed in the score so that they would occur after an interval, thus offering lighter 'entertainment' to follow coffee, brandy and cigars.

Cadence (sometimes 'close') A melodic and/or harmonic progression that brings a musical phrase, movement or whole work to rest, and therefore to a satisfyingly logical conclusion.

Cantata A work for chorus and/or soloists with orchestral/instrumental accompaniment. It is often, though not exclusively, on a sacred text, but is shorter than an oratorio.

Chorale (Ger. 'Choral') A metrically regular hymn-tune, used in Lutheran church services.

Chromatic A chromatic scale uses all the notes of the octave playable on a keyboard. Chromatic music refers to a style in which melodies and/or harmonies use notes that are 'foreign' to the familiar major or minor scales, and the parts often move in semitone steps.

Ensemble (Fr.) In an operatic ensemble, a section in which several soloists sing together, each singing a separate line, and perhaps also different words.

Forte (It.) Originally 'strong', nowadays usually 'loud'.

Grand Opera A somewhat imprecise term, usually meaning either 'serious' opera (as distinct from comic opera or operetta) or opera that is entirely sung. In French 'grand opéra' signifies a large-scale work, often on a historical or quasi-historical subject, in four or five acts, featuring a ballet and making extensive use of the chorus.

Leitmotif (Ger. and sometimes Eng. 'Leitmotiv') Literally 'leading motif'. In Wagner's music dramas it refers to a short theme, melodic phrase or chord sequence that represents a character, idea or emotion.

Libretto (It.) Literally 'little book'. The verbal text of a vocal work, especially an opera.

Mezzo-forte (also written by Wagner as 'Mezzoforte') 'Half-loud'.

Motet A short work for unaccompanied chorus, usually for use in church services.

Music Drama Term used by Wagner for his operas, from the *Ring* onwards, to emphasize the parity of the musical and dramatic elements.

Number A self-contained piece or section (for example an aria, duet or ensemble) forming part of an opera or oratorio, so called because each of these pieces is numbered separately in the score. A 'number opera' is therefore an opera in which the music is clearly divided up into separate sections.

Ornament Decoration or embellishment added to a melody to make it more florid or curvaceous.

Overture A piece of instrumental music that precedes an opera, oratorio or theatre play. In his music dramas Wagner preferred the more Romantic 'Prelude' (Ger. 'Vorspiel').

Piano (It.) 'Soft' or 'quiet'.

Program/ Programmatic Music which takes its character, and perhaps also elements of its form, from a literary source, or possibly from one of the visual arts.

Recitative Singing which directly imitates the melodic patterns and rhythms of speech (that is, 'recited'). In number opera, recitative sections are usually separate from the more melodic arias, duets, ensembles etc.

Sonata Extensive composition, usually in three or more movements, for solo instrument or small group of instruments.

Symphony Extensive orchestral composition, usually in four movements. The word 'symphonic' is sometimes used to indicate music in which the musical argument or drama is self-sufficient and self-explanatory.

Tempo (It.) 'Time'. The basic pulse or speed of a piece of music.

Time signature A sign – for instance 3/4, 4/4, 6/8 – placed at the beginning of a piece of music or musical section to indicate the number of beats per bar, and sometimes also the subdivision of those beats.

Tremolo (It.) 'Shaking, 'trembling'. In string playing, the rapid movement of the bow backwards and forwards across a string to create a fluttering or hazy effect.

Trill A rapid alternation between two adjacent notes.

Wagner tuba Brass instrument created by Wagner after he saw similar instruments in the workshops of Adolphe Sax (inventor of the saxophone), for use in his *Ring* cycle. Wagner tubas are more like deeper-pitched horns than tubas, and their parts are normally taken by horn players.

Annotations of CD Tracks

CD 1

[1] **Der fliegende Holländer.** Overture

The Overture to *Der fliegende Holländer* ('The Flying Dutchman') is a thrilling curtain-raiser for the opera, but it can also stand alone as a 'symphonic poem', distilling the opera's dramatic essence. At first we hear the raw, elemental voice of nature: roaring winds, lashing rain, surging waves – Wagner's experience of a storm at sea seems to have been translated directly into music. Then comes the quieter 'Redemption' theme (cor anglais), associated with the heroine, Senta. The storm resumes, leading to a more cheerful, major-key theme which in the opera accompanies the singing and dancing of the Norwegian sailors. The horns' fanfare theme from the opening (standing for the Dutchman himself) returns in triumph; but the last word is given to the 'Redemption' theme, magically transformed with liquid harp and soaring high strings.

[2] **Lohengrin.** Prelude

The opening of the Prelude to *Lohengrin* is a celebration of the glory of light. Bright major-key chords, high up on full violins, solo violin harmonics and woodwind cross-fade into one another ethereally. From this emerges the more rhythmically defined 'Grail' motif, at first on much-divided violins, then joined by full woodwind. Gradually the bass instruments enter, leading to a majestic full-orchestral climax, as though the Grail now stands completely revealed to the eyes of mortals. This depicts the descent of the Holy Grail from heavenly regions to the world of human beings, and two climactic cymbal clashes mark the high point of this revelation. Then the splendor fades as the Grail returns to the realms of light – as Lohengrin himself does at the end of the opera.

[3], [4] **Wesendonck Lieder**
No. 3: 'Im Treibhaus'
No. 5: 'Träume'
Wagner wrote his five *Wesendonck Lieder* for Mathilde Wesendonck, wife of his most important supporter during the years of his exile in Zurich. Their passionate love affair (possibly unconsummated) deeply colors this music, which sets poems by Mathilde. These two songs – both subtitled 'Study for *Tristan und Isolde*' – contain music that was to be reworked in the opera. No. 3, 'Im Treibhaus'

('In the Hothouse'), speaks of the longing of a plant for its native soil, stretching out its tendrils hopelessly into 'the empty horror of a desolate void'. No. 5, 'Träume' ('Dreams'), tells of the bliss that can only be found in the enchanted world of the imagination. Its sighing two-note figure was to be used still more tellingly in the lovers' music at the heart of Act II of *Tristan*.

5 **Tristan und Isolde**
Act I: Prelude – Act III: Isolde's Liebestod

Unlike the Prelude to *Lohengrin* and the Overture to *Der fliegende Holländer*, the Prelude to *Tristan und Isolde* does not stand comfortably on its own as a self-contained concert item. In it the emotions of desire and unappeasable longing are explored more profoundly and movingly than in any other piece of western classical music; but at the end the exquisitely painful dissonance of the opening 'Desire' motif remains unresolved. One 'solution' that became popular in Wagner's lifetime was to link its ending to the music of Isolde's 'Liebestod' ('Love-death') from the end of *Tristan*. This music, sung in the opera by Isolde, rises in great waves to an ecstatic climax; then, at the very end, the dissonance of the 'Desire' is at last resolved into a radiant chord of B major, as Isolde finds in death an end to her longing.

6 **Rienzi.** Overture

A great hit at its premiere in 1842, Wagner's early opera *Rienzi* is rarely performed today. The Overture is a useful 'sampler', however, as well as being very satisfying in its own right. The beginning shows Wagner's flair for ear-catching openings – the kind of thing that might make a theatre audience stop talking at once and listen hard. A single note on a trumpet swells from *pianissimo* to *forte* and back again, answered by mysterious low strings. Soon afterwards the full strings play the wonderful melody of Rienzi's prayer at the beginning of Act V. The exhilarating *Allegro* that follows reflects the mood of pomp and ceremony present throughout the opera.

7–11 **Die Walküre.** Act III, Scene 3 (Conclusion)

In the great final scene of *Die Walküre*, Wotan pronounces sentence on his disobedient daughter Brünnhilde (Track 7): she shall lie defenceless in sleep, prey to the first man who finds her. She appeals to his love for her, asking that protecting fire may surround her so that only a hero may reach her. Moved, Wotan concedes (Track 8). Sadly he sings of his love and admiration for her (Track 9) then summons the fire-god Loge to create the wall of fire (Track 10), adding that whoever fears the tip of his spear shall never have her (Track 11). Several important motifs are heard and developed in this scene. Listen out for the following: Wotan's sentence of 'Magic Sleep' (Track 7: 1.25, wind and string harmonies), the first foreshadowing of 'Brünnhilde's Slumber' (7: 2.07, strings), 'Siegfried' (7: 2.29, voice and orchestra), 'Wotan's Spear' (7: 3.08, wind), 'The Valkyries' (7: 3.23, trumpet), 'Loge' or 'Fire' (7: 3.23, orchestra), and, at the end, 'Fate' (Track 11: 3.27, brass).

CD 2

[1] **Die Meistersinger von Nürnberg.** Prelude

The Prelude to *Die Meistersinger* begins with a strong theme for full orchestra, reflecting the noble tradition of the Guild of Mastersingers – and perhaps also a little of the Masters' self-satisfaction. Gentler flutes and clarinets hint at the young nobleman Walther's love for the beautiful Eva, then a splendid march tune leads to an equally splendid song-theme for full orchestra: in Ernest Newman's words, 'the honest breasts of the Nuremberg burghers swelling with pride'. The key changes, and strings delicately foreshadow the melody with which Walther will eventually win the Mastersong competition. Lively woodwind suggests the merry-making of the young apprentices, before Wagner fuses all these themes in a triumphant contrapuntal display.

[2], [3] **Lohengrin**
Act II, Scene 4: Bridal Procession
Act III: Prelude

Despite its ethereal beginning, *Lohengrin* is the most tragic of Wagner's mature operas. Although *Der fliegende Holländer* and *Tannhäuser* end with the deaths of both hero and heroine, there is the overwhelming sense that sacrifice has brought redemption. In *Lohengrin* the reconciliation of the heavenly and the human – symbolized by the marriage of Lohengrin and Elsa – is ultimately thwarted. This is made all the more poignant by Wagner's music, which seems to invest so much hope in Elsa and Lohengrin's union. Listening to the magnificent, stately Bridal Procession from Act II and the brilliant orchestral introduction to Act III, one might never guess that fate has decided against the expected happy ending. Enjoyable as these two extracts are in their own right, they also show Wagner's growing mastery of dramatic irony.

[4] **Eine Faust-Ouvertüre**

Originally planned as the first movement of a huge 'dramatic symphony', *Eine Faust-Ouvertüre* ('A Faust Overture') stands alone as a powerful symphonic poem in its own right, as Wagner eventually realized. While the work still owes something to the example of Beethoven's Ninth Symphony, its dramatic thinking is not at all derivative. The opening, with its sinister theme for bass tuba, sounding through smoky string phrases, is a brilliant inspiration, and the anguished violin theme that emerges soon afterwards is no less impressive. From this emerges an *Allegro* with a powerful tragic momentum. The anguished violin theme (Faust himself?) is almost the first thing to be heard, but then quiet wind instruments turn the harmony from dark minor to bright major – almost certainly a foretaste of Faust's eventual redemption, as portrayed in Goethe's great verse drama.

5 **Parsifal.** Act I: Prelude

The Prelude to *Parsifal* is even more spacious and timeless in effect than the *Lohengrin* Prelude. The long, chant-like opening theme for muted strings and low woodwind is ingeniously written so that it seems to float free of the beat. After this come the swishing string and pulsating woodwind chords that suggest light from within. The gigantic opening paragraph is repeated, then brass quietly sound the noble 'Dresden Amen'. Later, horns and trumpets proclaim the majestic motif of 'Faith', rising in sequence then descending to the depths again. More anguished music tells of the suffering of Amfortas, and of the spear wound that caused it; but at the end the Prelude returns to the timeless peace of its opening. In the concert version performed here, the Dresden Amen pronounces a final blessing.

6, 7 **Tannhäuser**
Overture
Venusberg Music

Wagner's *Tannhäuser* Overture is most often heard in its original 'Dresden' version as a self-sufficient orchestral piece: there the opening Pilgrims' Chorus (first heard quietly on winds, then growing to a grand climax) returns to build a stirringly positive conclusion. In the revised 'Paris' score, however, the Overture sweeps onwards, straight into the music of the bacchanalian orgy that opens Act I. This revised continuation starts at the beginning of Track 7. The music of the new Venusberg scene is magnificent, but for some Wagnerians it is too close to the sound-world of *Tristan und Isolde* to sit comfortably with the earlier music of the Overture. So, does it work or not – and was Wagner right to consider revising it again at the end of his life? Judge for yourself.

8 – 10 **Götterdämmerung.** Act III, Scene 3 (Conclusion)

The end of Wagner's *Ring* cycle is – as it has to be – both emotionally overwhelming and a triumphant musical resolution. Brünnhilde signals to the vassals to lift Siegfried's body onto the funeral pyre and takes the ring from his finger (Track 8). She now knows it is her destiny to sacrifice herself and cleanse the ring by fire. She tells Wotan's ravens to fly to Valhalla with the message that the end of the gods is come (Track 9). Singing of her love for Siegfried, she mounts her horse and rides into the fire. The fire seems to fill the skies and the Rhine overflows, bearing the Rhinemaidens on its waves (Track 10). With a cry, Hagen tries to get the ring, but he is dragged under. Flosshilde appears bearing the ring in triumph, as Valhalla appears in the sky in flames. Motifs: 'Decline of the Gods' (Track 8: 0.19, woodwind and strings), 'River Rhine' (8: 0.27, orchestra), 'Rhinemaidens' (8: 0.57, clarinets, continued by violins), 'Dark Power of the Ring' (8: 2.09, woodwind) combined with 'The Curse' (8: 2.14, brass), 'Wotan's Spear' (9: 0.02, brass), 'Loge'/'Fire' (9: 0.15, orchestra), 'The Valkyries' (9: 1.30, horns), 'Redemption' or 'New-born Hope' (9: 1.59, voice and orchestra), 'Valhalla' (10: 1.41, brass).

Index

Author's Acknowledgments

Naming everyone to whom I owe insight or help in coming to terms with Wagner would require a small book in itself, not to mention a prodigious memory, so sincere apologies to anyone who may feel they have been unfairly left out. I should however single out the following: composers Alexander Goehr, Robin Holloway, Gerard McBurney, James MacMillan, Bayan Northcott, Geoffrey Poole, Poul Ruders, Robert Simpson and Hugh Wood; conductors Daniel Barenboim, Sir Simon Rattle and Wolfgang Sawallisch; writers and academics Paul Banks, Otto Biba, John Deathridge, Rüdiger Görner, Ivan Hewitt, David Nice, Richard Osborne and Derek Watson.

Special thanks are due to Wagner's biographer Barry Millington, who supplied much useful information and helped to shape my more general impressions, and to my teenage friend David Ashurst, whose irrepressible passion for playing huge chunks of Wagner (especially the Ring), as well as expatiating on their plots and central themes, gave me an invaluable early grounding. I would also like to thank my wife Kate who, despite her understandable reservations at the thought of my filling the house with Wagner's music for months on end, eventually conceded that the project was a valuable thing to have undertaken, and – as so often – had penetrating insights of her own to offer.

Thanks also to Genevieve Helsby and Nicolas Soames at Naxos for encouraging me to take up this project in the first place. Without that I might have found the idea of wrestling with this gigantic figure, and then trying to condense him into a relatively short, approachable introduction, just too daunting. If only for my sake, I am glad they prevailed.